THE STUDENT AS NIGGER

•

Essays and Stories

•

by Jerry Farber

PUBLISHED BY POCKET BOOKS NEW YORK

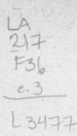
THE STUDENT AS NIGGER

Contact Books edition published August, 1969
Pocket Book edition published September, 1970

This *Pocket Book* edition includes every word
contained in the original, higher-priced edition. It is printed
from brand-new plates made from completely reset, clear, easy-to-read
type. *Pocket Book* editions are published by Pocket Books, a division
of Simon & Schuster, Inc., 630 Fifth Avenue, New York, N.Y. 10020.
Trademarks registered in the United States and other countries.

FOR MADDIE

ACKNOWLEDGMENTS

Thank you Judy Eisenstein Bagai, Woodrow Coleman, Maddie Farber and Peter Marin.

And thank you Walter Appling, Ayuko Babu, Bess Blanchette, Basil Busacca, Joe Butler, Rita Davis, James Eayrs, Les Farber, Bill Fick, Bill Fox, Paul Goodman, The Grateful Dead, Danny Gray, Byron Guyer, Robert Hall, Charlie Hamilton, Bruce Hartford, Roberta Krinsky, Timothy Leary, Dennis Lee, Anita Liebman, A.S. Neill, Bob Paskin, Fred Patten, Jan Popper, Elizabeth Sewell, Steve Sherman, W.D. Snodgrass, Theodore Sturgeon and Steve Tuttle.

CONTENTS

THE STUDENT
AS NIGGER

PREFACE

Early in 1967 I wrote "The Student As Nigger" and published it in the *Los Angeles Free Press*. The article was an outgrowth of my attempts to be a good teacher. After several years in the English department at L.A. State College, I had decided that there were limits to how well you could teach in an authoritarian and de-humanized school system. So I thought I would do my bit to help change the system.

When "The Student As Nigger" appeared, I hoped that a few other underground papers would pick it up but I had no idea that it would arouse the interest that it did. The article, particularly its central metaphor, embodied ideas and feelings that had been around for a long time but were then working their way rapidly up to the surface. I don't know exactly how often it has been reprinted; I would guess about 500 times. It has appeared in several magazines, in a book, in almost all of the underground papers and, most frequently, in student newspapers and pamphlets on hundreds of campuses in the United States and Canada.

The article has left a wake of trouble behind it— trouble that neatly illustrates its argument. For example: two high-school teachers in the Los Angeles area were fired on the spot for reading it to their classes. A Southern California state senator wrote a newspaper editorial attacking it as an "almost incredible abuse"; the article was subsequently debated in the state legis-lature's education committee. Campus editors who have reprinted it have routinely been called on the adminis-tration carpet. Frequently schools where "The Student

As Nigger" has appeared have themselves come under attack from the surrounding community. At one college a parent who had read it became so furious when he heard I was scheduled to speak there that he got 5000 signatures on a (unsuccessful) petition to keep me off campus.

At the University of Montana the article was used in a Freshman English class and was promptly attacked by an ROTC colonel, whose daughter was in the class. The colonel sent faculty members copies of the article, in which he had underlined all the objectionable words —all the way down to such modest vulgarities as "rat's ass." To my surprise the colonel even underlined "provo" (I suppose that, not knowing what it meant, he didn't want to take any chances). Interestingly enough, though the colonel's delicate sensibilities required him to underline "student-faculty lovemaking" and "goddamn school," it never occurred to him to underline "nigger." Before long the article became a major issue in a state-wide campaign to defeat a higher-education tax levy referendum. Thousands of copies were mailed to voters. Accompanying material urged citizens to vote down the referendum (it squeaked by) in protest and referred to "The Student As Nigger" as a "dirty, filthy source of moral poison," "degenerate writing" and "obscene pornographic smut" (the three biggies here in one memorable phrase).

In Canada "The Student As Nigger" was reprinted intact in the Hansard (official record) of the Canadian Parliament by an angry M.P., who described it in a speech to the Senate as a "suppurating sore in the body politic" and as "probably the worst piece of writing in a moral sense that has ever gone into a Senate Hansard."

I have received scarcely any criticism from students on the article. In fact, it seems that there is little in "The Student As Nigger" that most students don't already know very well. Students, and a number of teachers as well, have welcomed it as an expression of their anger, their frustration and their growing desire for change. The outraged criticism has come primarily from administrators, parents and elected officials—and this outrage has centered not so much on the ideas in the article as on its "filthy language." There is little I can say in answer to this kind of criticism. I don't believe that any words are filthy, not even words like "counterinsurgency," and certainly not words like "fuck," "pussy," "cock" and so on. In any case, I would never censor anything I wrote just as I would never censor my speech in the classroom. I don't go out of my way, as some persons have assumed, to use so-called taboo words but, on the other hand, I don't go out of my way to avoid them. They simply occur where they want to, as do other words in the language. In "The Student As Nigger," the diction I used was very much a part of what I was trying to say—so much so that I have had to refuse dozens of reprint requests (including one from the *New York Times*) which would have involved cutting out a number of salty phrases.

When people have criticized the ideas in "The Student As Nigger," they have tended to accuse me of advocating educational anarchy. This would be both a respectable and an intriguing position but it is not mine. Lately, I've noticed, when you attack existing structures, you are accused of advocating that there be no structures at all. Certainly it is not anarchy to say that students and teachers should run their own schools. Nor is it anarchy to want to do away with the grading system and similar claptrap. The phrase "campus anarchy," which we hear a good deal nowadays, appeals to a familiar kind of psychological hangup. When you're bound up tight, any change or loosening seems to threaten anarchy. To persons in such a position, the choice often appears limited to one between iron restraint and total abandon (whatever that means).

As time passes, my attitude toward "The Student As Nigger" changes. I still like it and I'm glad I wrote it —but the article has moved away from the center of my thoughts about school and has come to occupy a more peripheral position. When I wrote it, I was concerned mainly with the relationship between students and teachers, with their respective roles. Since then I have thought a great deal about the institutional framework within which these roles are acted out and, even more, about the still larger social framework within which our schools exist.

The analogy with which I began seems more appropriate than I realized at the time. Originally I saw students as niggers and slaves primarily in relation to their teachers and administrators. Now I realize more clearly than before that students are *society's* slaves and that teachers are no more than overseers. It's a mistake to get hung up exclusively in a struggle against teachers just as it's a mistake to let one's anger toward ghetto cops obscure the larger threat of the racist society that pays their salary and buys their bullets.

For the past two years I have been trying to see as deeply as I could into our schools and to work out an analysis of them that would take into account their intertwined cause-effect relationship with the surrounding society. The result of this effort is "The Student and Society," which opens this book.

The essay which follows it, "The Four-Fold Path," is a partial and tentative answer to the question which I have been asked most often when speaking to students: what can a person do to change the educational system? I've included the article because I thought it might be useful but I have some doubts. Students who ask "What can I do?" usually aren't ready. When they're ready, they don't need to be told what to do.

The second part of this book is not at all about school, yet the essays and stories in it are, to me, quite in the same spirit as the first part. The very last piece, for example, "Hancock Park in Late December," was written with no thought of school; yet it embodies a kind of feeling, I think, that we rarely get in school now but that we ought to and, hopefully, will get when our schools are straightened out or, perhaps, replaced with something else entirely.

THE STUDENT AND SOCIETY:

AN ANNOTATED MANIFESTO

School is where you let the dying society put its trip on you. Our schools may seem useful: to make children into doctors, sociologists, engineers—to discover things. But they're poisonous as well. They exploit and enslave students; they petrify society; they make democracy unlikely. And it's not *what* you're taught that does the harm but *how* you're taught. Our schools teach you by pushing you around, by stealing your will and your sense of power, by making timid square apathetic slaves out of you—authority addicts.

Schooling doesn't have to be this destructive. If it weren't compulsory, if schools were autonomous and were run by the people in them, then we could learn without being subdued and stupefied in the process. And, perhaps, we could regain control of our own society.

Students can change things if they want to because they have the power to say "no." When you go to school, you're doing society a favor. And when you say "no," you withhold much more than your attendance. You deny continuity to the dying society; you put the future on strike. Students can have the kind of school they want—or even something else entirely if they want—because there isn't going to be any school at all without them.

17

NOTES

(1) "SCHOOL IS WHERE YOU LET THE DYING
SOCIETY PUT ITS TRIP ON YOU."

School is a genetic mechanism for society, a kind of
DNA process that continually recreates styles, skills,
values, hangups—and so keeps the whole thing going.
The dying part of society—the society that has been—
molds the emerging part more or less in its own image,
and fashions the society that will be.

Schooling also makes change possible—evolution, if
you like. But here we run into a problem. Although our
schools foster enormous technological change, they help
to keep social change within very narrow limits. Thanks
to them, the technological capacity of society evolves at
an explosive rate. But there is no comparable, adaptive
evolution in the overall social framework, nor in the
consciousness of the individuals who make up society. It
isn't just that schools fail to create the necessary social
change. They actually restrain it. They prevent it.
(*How* they prevent it is the subject of the Notes that
follow.)

When I say that schools serve the society-that-has-
been, the dying society, I mean just that. It isn't "society" itself that runs our schools. Children and adolescents are a huge segment of society but they don't
run schools. Even young adults don't run them. Nor
as a general rule do workers. Nor do black people
(although a few Negroes do). Nor do the poor in
general. By and large our schools are in the hands of
the most entrenched and rigidly conservative elements
in society. In the secondary and elementary schools,
students, of course, have no power and teachers have
little power. Administrators possess somewhat more, but
the real control comes from those solid Chamber-of-
Commerce types—those priests of the American Way—

on the school board. They uphold the sovereignty of the past; they are the very avatars of institutional inertia. As for the colleges and universities, California, where I teach, is typical. Higher education is controlled primarily by the business elite, aided by a sprinkling of aging politicos, venerable clergymen and society matrons.* And in the rare cases when these trustees and governing boards relax their tight control, they are backstopped by our elected officials, whose noses are always aquiver for subversion and scandal and who are epitomized in that querulous Mrs. Grundy, our current governor.

While schools stifle social change, technological change is, to repeat, another matter. The society-that-has-been, in its slavering pursuit of higher profits and better weapons, demands technological progress at a fantastic, accelerating rate. Universities have consequently become a giant industry in their own right. A few tatters of commencement-day rhetoric still cling to them but it becomes more obvious every day that the modern university is not much more than a Research, Development and Training center set up to service government and industry. And so we have a technological explosion within the rigid confines of our unchanging social institutions and values. Schools today give us fantastic power at the same time as they sap our ability to handle it. Good luck, everybody.

(2) "IT'S NOT *WHAT* YOU'RE TAUGHT THAT DOES THE HARM BUT *HOW* YOU'RE TAUGHT."

In fact, for most of your school life, it doesn't make that much difference what subject you're taught. The

---

* Read James Ridgeway's "The Closed Corporation: American Universities in Crisis" (New York, 1968). Ridgeway provides extensive information on the interlocking managements of universities and major corporations, as well as an analysis of the "big-business" aspect of the universities themselves.

real lesson is the method. The medium in school truly is the message. And the medium is, above all, coercive. You're forced to attend. The subjects are required. You *have* to do homework. You *must* observe school rules. And throughout, you're bullied into docility and submissiveness. Even modern liberal refinements don't really help. So you're called an underachiever instead of a dummy. So they send you to a counselor instead of beating you. It's still not your choice to be there. They may pad the handcuffs—but the handcuffs stay on.

Which particular subject they happen to teach is far less important than the fact that it is required. We don't learn that much subject matter in school anyway in proportion to the huge part of our lives that we spend there. But what we do learn very well, thanks to the method, is to accept choices that have been made for us. Which rule they make you follow is less important than the fact that there are rules. I hear about English teachers who won't allow their students to begin a sentence with "and." Or about high schools where the male students are not permitted to wear a T-shirt unless it has a pocket. I no longer dismiss such rules as merely pointless. The very point to such rules is their pointlessness.

The true and enduring content of education is its method. The method that currently prevails in schools is standardized, impersonal and coercive. What it teaches best is—itself. If, on the other hand, the method were individual, human and free, it would teach that. It would not, however, mesh smoothly into the machine we seem to have chosen as a model for our society.

It's how you're taught that does the harm. You may only study geometry for a semester—or French for two years. But *doing what you're told,* whether or not it makes sense, is a lesson you get every blessed school day for twelve years or more. You know how malleable we humans are. And you know what good learners we are—how little time it takes us to learn to drive a car or a plane or to play passable guitar. So imagine what the effect must be upon our apt and impression-able minds of a twelve-year course in servility. Think about it. Twelve years of tardy bells and hall passes; of graded homework, graded tests, graded conduct; of report cards, GPA's, honors lists, citizenship ratings; of dress codes, straight lines and silence. *What is it that they're teaching you?* Twelve years pitted against your classmates in a daily Roman circus. The game is Doing What You're Told. The winners get gold stars, affec-tion, envy; they get A's and E's, honors, awards and college scholarships. The losers get humiliation and deg-radation. The fear of losing the game is a great fear: it's the fear of swats, of the principal's office, and above all the fear of failing. What if you fail and have to watch your friends move past you to glory? And, of course, the worst could happen: you could be expelled. Not that very many kids get swats or fail or are ex-pelled. But it doesn't take many for the message to get across. These few heavy losers are like severed heads displayed at the city gates to keep the populace in line.

And, to make it worse, all of this pressure is aug-mented by those countless parents who are ego freaks and competition heads and who forcibly pass their ad-diction on to their kids. The pressure at school isn't enough; they *pay* the kids for A's and punish them for D's and F's.

But can you feel any of this? Can you understand what has been done to your mind? We get so used to the pressure that we scarcely are conscious of it with-out making some effort.

Why does the medium of education affect us so deeply while its purported content—the subject matter —so often slips our minds? This is partly because the content varies from year to year while the form remains more or less the same; but also because the form—a structure of rules, punishments, rewards—affects us di-rectly in a real way, while the subject matter may have no such immediate grasp on our lives. After all, don't we tend to learn best what matters most? Under a coercive system it isn't really the subject that matters;

what matters is pleasing the authorities. These two are far from the same thing.

Remember French class in high school (or college, for that matter)? The teacher calls on you, one at a time, to see if you've prepared the questions at the end of Leçon 19. "Marshall," she asks, *"qu'est-ce que Robert allait faire le mardi?"* Marshall doesn't get to respond that he doesn't give a shit—not even in French. Fat chance. While he's in school, he's got to be servile to stay out of trouble. And the law requires him to be in school. He's got to do the questions in Leçon 19 because the teacher said to. He's got to do what the teacher said in order to pass the course. He's got to pass the course to get to college. He's got to get to college because it's been explained to him that he'll be a clod all his life if he doesn't; at assembly they've put up charts showing how many hundreds of thousands of dollars more he'll make in his lifetime if he goes to college. And, of course, there's an immediate reason as well for Marshall to have done his homework. If he hasn't, he'll be embarrassed in front of the class.

The educational medium has a very real hold on his life. Unfortunately, the subject probably does not. So we can't console him for all this dull toil by pointing out that he is at least learning French. Because, of course, he isn't. He'll take two years of French in high school. And when he gets to college, it will be like they never happened. Right? In fact, some acquaintances from Montreal recently told me that English-speaking students there are required to take French every year from the second grade on. And yet, I was told, after ten years of the language, they still haven't learned it.

Or what about Freshman English? What actually gets taught? The purported subject matter is usually writing. But consider, up front, who teaches the course. It's usually some well-meaning instructor or TA whose own writing achievements have reached their zenith in a series of idle and heroically dull papers, written in pretentious faggot-academic for his graduate classes. And how does he teach? What's his method? Well, that depends—because things are changing. Somewhere in some college there is undoubtedly a heavyweight, on the verge of being fired, who is teaching silence to freshmen so that they can hear themselves. Maybe somewhere else a teacher has renounced grading and is letting the students write what they want. Most Freshman English teachers, however, are doing the standard thing. They're demanding and then grading "themes" on capital punishment and on lowering the voting age. They're compelling students to drudge through topic-sentence exercises, outline exercises, library exercises, inference-judgment-report exercises, and a flood of other dreary busy work. They think they know the difference between a B minus essay and a C plus essay, and they teach their students to believe in such foolishness. They "correct" their students' work with *ex cathedra* judgments, none of which a student is at liberty to ignore.

In Freshman English, the method teaches you—in case you haven't already gotten the message—that writing is a drag. It's a job you do to please someone else (God knows that writing a theme on The Vanishing Individualist is hardly your own idea of how to spend Sunday night) Writing is school work and "English" is learning how to please your English teacher. What interest there is in the course is provided not so much by your writing experience as by the method. That is to say, you may write something tonight but the payoff, the real excitement, won't come until next week when the papers are handed back and you can find out "what you got." That's what makes it all worthwhile; that's what school writing is all about: pleasing the teacher.

The very essence of Freshman English is that term paper they force out of you. In perfect order, impeccably footnoted, unreal and totally useless—that term paper, that empty form, is pretty much the content of the course: submission—alienation—learning to live a pretend intellectual life, pretend-caring about pretend things.

Sometimes you even get a pretend choice; you're allowed to pick your own topic. But you don't get to make the one choice that would give the whole business some meaning: the choice to write no paper at all. Oh, you *can* make that choice. But then you don't get through Freshman English, which means you don't get through college and, therefore, don't get your hands in the gigantic goodie-box which is programmed to open only upon insertion of a college diploma. Or maybe you even get drafted right away. Yeah, you've got a hell of a choice. And college teachers like to style themselves "seekers after truth." Sure. "Know the truth and the truth shall get you a B." The truth in a freshman term paper is about the same truth a banker can expect from his shoeshine boy.

I'm sorry to sound so snotty about composition teachers. God knows, I've been there too. In my first year I even assigned research papers in Freshman English. I didn't really want to but I did it anyway "to prepare students for their other courses." I prepared them all right. My method was the term paper. What I taught was alienation and servility. Now I try to *un*prepare students for their other courses. I only wish I were better at it.

The medium of schooling, by the way, covers much more than assignments, grading, rules and so on. If *how* you're taught exerts a profound effect, what about the physical environment? What does a classroom teach?

Consider how most classrooms are set up. Everyone is turned toward the teacher and away from his classmates. You can't see the faces of those in front of you; you have to twist your neck to see the persons behind you. Frequently, seats are bolted to the floor or fastened together in rigid rows. This classroom, like the grading system, isolates students from each other and makes them passive receptacles. All the action, it implies, is at the front of the room.

What would be better? A circle? For a while I used to ask classes to sit in a circle (in rooms where we weren't bolted down). It was much better. But after a time I become depressed about it. It was still awkwardly geometrical; it was still my trip, and they were still dutifully following orders. I felt that if I told them to sit on each other's heads, they'd do it. So next semester I simply took a position in the second seat of the fourth row or thereabouts. I still do this most of the time. Some classes begin to move their chairs around, often within a matter of days, into a sort of loose, pleasant jumble, although they usually maintain a certain pious distance from me, leaving me at the center of a small but unmistakable magic circle. Occasionally, a class is unbelievably faithful to the traditional seating plan. They sit mournfully facing an empty altar and they sprain their necks trying to see me and the other students. I curse and mutter but they hold firm. It's almost as though they're saying, "Screw you, you bastard, you're going to have to *tell* us to move." And I swear to myself I won't. But I usually give in about half way through the semester.

But why those chairs at all? Why forty identical desk-chairs in a bleak, ugly room? Why should school have to remind us of jail or the army? (A rhetorical question, I'm afraid.) For that matter, why are there classrooms? Suppose we started over from scratch. What would be a good place to learn stress analysis? What would be a good place to study Zen? To learn about child development? To learn Spanish? To read poetry? You know, wherever I've seen classrooms, from UCLA to elementary schools in Texas, it's always the same stark chamber. The classrooms we have are a nationwide chain of mortuaries. What on earth are we trying to teach?

The scariest thing about a classroom is that it acts as a sort of psychological switch. You walk into a classroom; some things switch on in you and others switch off. All sorts of weird unreal things start to happen. Any teacher who has tried simply to be real in a classroom knows what I'm talking about. This is so hard to express . . . you walk in and everyone's face is a mask.

Last semester I had the best room yet. Because of overcrowding, one class was in an apartment living room on the edge of campus. The school did its well-meaning best to kill the room, boarding up the door to the kitchen and the can and literally filling the small room with long formica-topped grammar-school tables (the formica itself is a message: furniture has won; you ain't carving no initials in these desks, baby). For a while we floundered miserably but then things got better. Sometimes we sat in a big square. Sometimes we sat on top of the tables; once we crawled under them where it was dark and restful. Sometimes we'd pile up the tables and sit in a bunch on the carpet. Sometimes we'd sit on the grass outside. It was only a very small gain though. Given our conditioning and the overall college context, I could have held that class at the beach, at home, in the Avalon Ballroom. I would still be *holding* it; they would still want to rest limply in my hands—good natured, obedient students. Neither they nor I can get out from under our schooling so quickly as we might like.

I think that what we need is not to touch up or modernize classrooms but rather to eliminate them.

(Question from the audience: "Where would we learn?" Answer: "We'd manage.")

(3) "THEY EXPLOIT AND ENSLAVE STUDENTS; THEY PETRIFY SOCIETY . . ."

Let me not be accused of ignoring "what's right with" our schools—to use the patriotic jargon. Schools are where you learn to read, write sort of, and do long division. Everyone knows about that. In college you learn about Pavlov, mitosis, Java Man and why we fought the Civil War. You may forget about Java Man but you get to keep your degree just the same, and it gets you a job. College is also where they discover new medicines, new kinds of plastic and new herbicides to use in Asia. But everybody knows all that. I want to return to the exploit-enslave-and-petrify part.

It's ironic. Radicals dream midnight police raids, or sit around over coffee and talk with glittering eyes about Repression—about those internment camps that are waiting empty. And all the time Miss Jones does her quiet thing with the kids in third grade.

People like to chat about the fascist threat or the communist threat. But their visions of repression are for the most part romantic and self indulgent: massacres, machine guns drowning out La Marseillaise. And in the meantime someone stops another tenth grader for a hall-pass check and notices that his T-shirt doesn't have a pocket on it. In the meantime the Bank of America hands out another round of high-school achievement awards. In the meantime I grade another set of quizzes.

God knows the real massacres continue. But the machine gun isn't really what is to be feared most in our civilized Western world. It just isn't needed all that much. The kids leave Miss Jones' class. And they go on to junior high and high school and college. And most of them will never need to be put in an internment camp. Because they're already there. Do you think I'm overstating it? That's what's so frightening: we have the illusion that we're free.

In school we learn to be good little Americans—or Frenchmen—or Russians. We learn how to take the crap that's going to be shoveled on us all our lives. In school the state wraps up people's minds so tight that it can afford to leave their bodies alone.

Repression? You want to see victims of repression? Come look at most of the students at San Diego State College, where I work. They *want* to be told what to do. They don't know how to be free. They've given their will to this institution just as they'll continue to give their will to the institutions that engulf them in the future.

Schools exploit you because they tap your power and use it to perpetuate society's trip, while they teach you not to respect your own. They turn you away from yourself and toward the institutions around you. Schools petrify society because their method, characterized by coercion from the top down, works against any substantial social change. Students are coerced by teachers, who take orders from administrators, who do the bidding of those stalwarts of the status quo on the board of education or the board of trustees. Schools petrify society because students, through them, learn how to adjust unquestioningly to institutions and how to exercise their critical thought only within narrow limits prescribed by the authorities. In fact, as long as a heavy preponderance of a nation's citizens are "good students" and are in some way rewarded for their performance, then dissenters and radical thinkers are no threat and can be permitted to express their opinions relatively unmolested. In the United States, free expression, to the extent that we have it, is a luxury commodity made available by the high standard of living and by the efficient functioning of such disguised forms of repression as schooling.

Schools preserve the status quo in two complementary ways: by molding the young and by screening them. Today almost all of the positions of relative power in the United States are reserved for those who have completed the full sixteen-year treatment, and perhaps a little more. Persons who are unwilling to have their minds and bodies pushed around incessantly are less likely to get through and therefore tend to be screened out of the power centers; the persons who do get through are more likely to accept things as they are and to make their own contributions in "safe" areas. Thus corporations and government agencies insist that executive trainees have a bachelor's degree, often without specifying any particular major. The degree, therefore, doesn't represent any particular body of knowledge. What *does* it represent? A certain mentality.

It is true, though, that an increasing number of rebels and freaks are getting through (as well as a much larger number of essentially adjusted students who try to have the best of two worlds by pretending that they are rebels and freaks). The small but noisy student rebellion of recent years has had the effect of bringing to campus a number of drop-ins—dissidents who would not otherwise be there. One friend of mine is an excellent example. He belonged to a Trotskyist youth group as a teenager but threw that over in 1963 because the civil rights movement seemed to be accomplishing more than his youth group was. He had made a few futile attempts at college but realized that he had absolutely no interest in it and furthermore had no time for it. After a couple of years in Los Angeles, he disappeared into the Southern movement: Alabama, Mississippi, Georgia. For a while I lost track of him. Then, last year, I heard from him again; he had just enrolled in San Francisco State College—where the action is. He is typical of a growing minority of students; he may do more or less what's needed to stay in school but he is more than willing to risk being expelled or failed out (two years ago he was risking his life). It is unlikely that college will disarm him.

As the tensions in our society work their way up to the surface, some overt rebellion appears in many settings; certainly it appears in schools, which offer at least a meeting place and staging ground for young middle-class rebels. May it grow in good health. But, as our college presidents are fond of pointing out, the great majority—the great silent majority—are there "not to make trouble but to get an education" (for "education," read "degree").

What about this majority? What is the mentality which employers depend upon our school system to deliver? What is most likely to emerge from the sixteen-year molding and screening process?

Well, a "good citizen" of sorts—isn't that the way they put it on report cards? Thoroughly schooled and ready for GE or IBM or the State Department, the

graduate is a skilled, neat, disciplined worker with just
enough initiative to carry out fairly complicated assignments but not so much initiative that he will seriously
question the assignment itself. He is affably but fiercely
competitive with his peers and he is submissive to his
superiors. In fact, as long as he has some respect
from his peers and subordinates, he is willing to be almost naked of dignity in the eyes of his superiors; there
is very little shit he will not eat if there is something
to be gained by it. In asserting himself he is moderate,
even timid—except when he exercises the power of a
great institution, when he himself is the superior, when
he puts on some kind of real or figurative uniform.
At that point he is likely to assume the sacerdotal mask
that his teachers wore. At that point—when he becomes
official—his jaw hardens.

This college graduate is positively addicted to rules
of all sorts at every level. In fact, should he help to
form some club or group, it will probably have by-laws
and officers and will follow parliamentary procedure.
Even in games—cards, Monopoly, whatever—he is
likely to have a passionate respect for the rules and to
get bent out of shape if their sanctity is violated.

Ever since his gold-and-silver-star days he has been
hooked on status and achievement symbol systems. He
has a hunter's eye for the nuances of such systems in
his work, in his leisure life and in the society at large.
He carries a series of grade-point averages in his head
and they rise or fall with an invitation to lunch, the
purchase of a Triumph TR-2, a friendly punch on the
arm from his ski instructor or the disrespectful attitude
of a bank teller.

Since grade school, also, he has known how to become mildly enthusiastic about narrow choices without
ever being tempted to venture rebelliously out of the
field of choice assigned to him. His political world, for
example, is peopled with Nixons and Humphreys; its
frontiers are guarded by McCarthys and Reagans. He
himself has had a taste of politics: he was elected
sophomore class president in college on a platform

that advocated extending snack-bar hours in the evening. Like Auden's "Unknown Citizen": when there is peace, he is for peace; when there is war, he goes. He doesn't expect a wide range to choose from in politics. His chief arena of choice is the marketplace, where he can choose enthusiastically among forty or fifty varieties of cigarette, without, incidentally, ever being tempted to choose the one variety that will turn him on. His drugs are still likely to be the orthodox ones, the consciousness-contractors: liquor, tranquilizers, a little TV.

He yearns for more free time but finds himself uncomfortable with very much of it. His vacations tend to be well structured. From time to time he feels oppressed and would like to "break out" but he isn't sure what that means. Leaving his family? Starting his own business? Buying a boat? He's not sure.

Let me stop at this point. There is, thank God, a limit to the meaningfulness of such a stereotyped characterization. It hits home in those areas where the college graduate has literally been stereotyped by his upbringing and by the rigid matrix of his schools. But it leaves out what makes him one individual, what makes him real. Doesn't he have a self beyond the stereotype? Isn't he unique—splendid—a center of existence? Isn't he, to use Timothy Leary's phrase, a two-billion-year-old carrier of the Light? Of course. But who sees it? His self has been scared into hiding. The stereotype that has been made of him hides his uniqueness, his inner life, his majesty from our eyes and, to a great extent from his own as well. He's got a sure A in Citizenship but he's failing in self-realization (a subject not too likely to appear in the curriculum).

Let's understand, when we consider this college graduate, that harm has been done not only to him but to society as well. There may, after all, be some of us who assume that dehumanization and standardization are no more than the price that an individual pays in return for a smoothly functioning society. But is that true? Is this man really what's good for society?

Social change is not just the radical's hang-up. It's a

means of adaptation, of self preservation. Now, as our technology and our environment change with increasing rapidity, as we acquire ever more awesome resources and more bewildering problems, we need the capacity to recreate our society continually rather than be victimized by it. This, of course, is the sort of thing that gets said a great deal nowadays but what doesn't get said is that we will not meet this need for rebirth without giving up what we now call schooling. A crisis in civilization—and we are in the midst of several—*demands* the radical thought, the radical will and the profound self-confidence which have been schooled out of our college-educated institutional man. His narrow vision and his submissive conformity aren't good for society; they paralyze it. They are a curse on it.

(4) "THEY MAKE DEMOCRACY UNLIKELY."

Our schools make democracy unlikely because they rob the people, who are supposed to be sovereign, of their sense of power and of their ability to will meaningful institutional changes.

The democratic ideal—to which even the most conservative college trustees usually give lip service—means government of, by and for the people. It means power in the hands of the people. Our schools, however, remain less suited to this ideal than to an authoritarian society; they are more effective in teaching obedience than in fostering freedom. Our textbooks may teach one kind of political system but the method by which our schools operate teaches another. And the method wins out over the textbooks overwhelmingly. A more substantial degree of democracy will become likely only when we understand that political freedom is not merely a constitutional matter; it's also a state of mind, which can be either nurtured or blighted in school.

I don't mean to ignore the reasons that already abound to explain that immense gap between our ideals of democracy and the system we see operating.

Some people, for example, argue that democracy only works well in small political units and that centralized democratic government of 200 million persons is just not possible. Others insist that the people are and will always remain too stupid and ill-informed to make political decisions. Then there's the very persuasive socialist argument: democracy is just not compatible with capitalism. Even if you grant the socialist proposition, though, the question remains: is democracy compatible with socialism? I think it could be, more or less—but there are problems involved that are not normally recognized in this kind of analysis.

A socialist country where schooling is standardized and coercive might well, in time, develop an electorate as dismal as ours *even though* its constitution provided the most extensive political freedom for the individual and even though it had eliminated class exploitation in the traditional sense. In fact, the resources adhering to a powerful socialist government create a very special danger in this area. That's why the growing student power movement has the greatest importance politically. The more that political radicalism comes to include educational radicalism, the more nearly attainable democratic government will be.

Capitalist or socialist, a democracy cannot possibly function if its citizens are educated to be clever robots. The way to educate children for democracy is to let them do it—that doesn't mean allowing them to practice empty forms, to make pretend decisions or to vote on trivia; it means that they participate in the real decisions that affect them. You learn democracy in school not by defining it or by simulating it but by doing it.

If students and teachers ran their own schools, it would do more for democracy than all the government classes ever taught. But it would have to be just that: true participation in running the schools. Not those little make-believe student governments which govern in about the same way that baby's toy steering wheel drives daddy's car. Not even anything like those "faculty senates," which retain the right to create college policy as long as they don't abuse that right by exercising it.

Also, in considering the effect of schooling on democracy, it's wise to think not only about the overall academic decision-making process but also about day-to-day classroom experience as well. That's at the very heart of the problem. It's in the classroom where you learn that happiness is submission and where you grow used to authoritarianism and coercion. It's in the classroom where you learn how to follow orders mindlessly and how to surrender your sovereignty to an institution.

Incidentally, in discussing this question, I've often heard the objection that teachers legitimately possess authority by virtue of their knowledge and that, therefore, democracy is out of place in the classroom. This argument is a favorite with teachers, so it deserves some attention.

It's true that many teachers possess authority in one particular sense of the word but that does not entitle them to authority in every sense of the word. A teacher's authority rests in his special knowledge or ability, not in his power over students. I may be, say, an authority in ancient history but what has that to do with authority in the sense of a right to enforce obedience, to reward and punish? And the fact that I work for the state of California doesn't amplify my academic authority. If I'm sound in my analysis of Athenian society, the state of California adds nothing. If I'm all wrong, the state of California doesn't make me less wrong.

Democracy in school doesn't mean that a class votes on whether two and two make four, even though that seems to be the fear of some teachers. Suppose, for example, my entire history class insists that Rome fell because of its sexual laxity. Suppose we argue. I give my reasons and they give theirs. Then, in desperation, I try to impress them by detailing my academic background but they still insist that they're right. In this (unlikely) situation what relevance would grading have? What would it add to my true authority if I were able to pass, fail, expel, what have you? My value to a class is that I can be of some kind of assistance to them. What they make of it is up to them. I'm a teacher not a cop.* Democracy in school doesn't mean that we vote on what's true; it means that education isn't anything which is *done to* somebody.

(5) "AUTHORITY ADDICTS"

It's time to say a few kind words about our coercive schools. They do—more or less—solve an existential problem. They shape time for us and thus give some meaning, if not to our life, then at least to some segments of it. Do you know what I mean? You study off and on for a final exam, slowly building tension as the date approaches. The night before, you get no sleep; you're in a strange world of glaring lights, notes, coffee cups, piled up books. Whatever other worries you might have are suspended. This task takes precedence; it's something to hold on to. When you approach the classroom, your exhaustion disappears in a fresh wave of tension and nervous energy. This all has to be important, has to be meaningful; anything you stay up all night for and get this worked up about has to mean something. And when you finish the bluebooks, they rest substantial on your desk. It wasn't all a dream; you've got the bluebooks and, eventually, the grade to prove it.

Courses may be pointless and uninteresting. The data may go through you like mineral oil. But at least it is some kind of challenge. And while you're involved in all this, time is off *your* hands and rests in *theirs*—the authorities'. Should you not be attending school, you

---

* One counter-argument might be that the authority to pass and fail is necessary, not to coerce knowledge, but to determine a student's fitness to enter a given field or profession. For a discussion of this question and of grading in general, "A Young Person's Guide to the Grading System."

may feel that you're pissing away time—days and weeks; you may begin to feel very uncomfortable. On your own, you have to face the responsibility for how you spend time. But in school you don't. What they make you do may obviously be a waste but at least the responsibility isn't charged to your account. School in this respect is, once again, like the army or jail. Once you're in, you may have all kinds of problems but freedom isn't one of them.

After you leave school and get a job, you'll find you *need* the job just as you learned to need school. You'll remain an existential minor who needs trustees to spend his time for him.

The schools we have are a cop-out. Why not face the responsibility for what we do with our time? And if we need structures to inform our time, why not find more congenial, more human ones. Why not surround ourselves with tailor-made educational structures rather than torture ourselves to fit the Procrustean set-up we have now.

Besides, things are changing. The leisure-time explosion is removing even the solace of constant work. Leisure calls on the ability to accept autonomy, to be content with internal justification for what you do. The more leisure we have, the more we need to be able to perceive our own needs and then to follow them for no other reason than that we want to.

So where are we headed? Are we going to face the existential problem or run from it? Will we let time fall on our very own hands without trying to kill it. Or will we continue to look for authorities to take the burden of our freedom from us. As we free ourselves from work in the traditional sense, we have the opportunity to lift our heads up and to look around; we become more free to create our lives rather than undergo them.

Drugs, by the way, have some relationship both to school and to the increase in leisure time. A growing number of people have found that smoking a little

weed helps them to appreciate the possibilities of un-
structured, uninstitutionalized time. Acid and the other
psychedelic drugs typically open up possibilities beyond
school and beyond the job (dropping out is always
dropping *in* to something else). The educational reform
movement probably owes a good deal to students and
teachers whose drug experiences have made them
impatient with the miserable use that schools make of
their time.

(6) "IF IT WEREN'T COMPULSORY . . ."

If we want our children locked up all day until
they're sixteen, let's at least be honest about it and stop
trying to pass imprisonment off as education.

Say, for example, that a mother and father would
like their eight-year-old boy out of the house all day
and also off the streets. Then I guess they will want
there to be some place for him to go. Call it a youth
center, a postgraduate nursery or a daytime internment
camp. But why does it have to be a school? It should
have plenty of room and lots of variety: places to be
alone if you want, places to play games if you want,
places to build things, and places to learn how to read
and do sums—*if you want*.

Learning isn't a duty that we must be flogged into
performing; it's our birthright, our very human specialty
and joy. Places to learn are everywhere. So are reasons
to learn. All we need, occasionally, is a little help from
our friends.

We don't need compulsory schooling to force us to
read. There are good reasons to read and things all
around us that want to be read. And if someone should
choose to pass his life illiterate, there are other communications media accessible to him. He'll probably
make out fine. He may even be able to teach the rest
of us some things that print hides.

It would be well if we stopped lying to ourselves
about what compulsory schooling does for our children.

It temporarily imprisons them; it standardizes them; it intimidates them. If that's what we want, we should admit it.

There's not much point in going on about this. If you've somehow missed reading A.S. Neill's *Summerhill,* you ought to go out and get it.

Incidentally, with compulsory schooling eliminated, there is no reason to assume that most parents will send their children to public internment centers during the day, or that learning itself will be as dependent upon public institutions as it now is. With compulsory education and all the related red tape out of the way, small groups of parents should be able to make their own arrangements to care for their children and even to satisfy the children's desire to learn. Some areas of learning—nuclear physics, for example—require heavy financial support. But many other areas do not; they provide opportunities for those who want to learn or teach to bypass official institutions. Furthermore, advances in computers, in information retrieval and in communication should soon make it much easier and cheaper than it is now to learn outside of public schools. Technological developments should, before long, give a home resources that are presently available only to a large and well-funded school. Sooner or later, if a child (or adult) wants to learn more about, say, snakes or jet engines, he should be able to tune in, at home, to books, films, learning computers and so on, which he can use as much or as little as he wants. Naturally, if the child chooses not to use the computers and books, that should be his unrestricted right. What I'm getting at is that parents should, before long, be able to develop a formidable alternative to our system of compulsory public elementary schools. As for older children—adolescents—the whole matter is less a parental responsibility and more their own.

(7) "IF SCHOOLS WERE AUTONOMOUS AND WERE RUN BY THE PEOPLE IN THEM . . ."

Learning is not something that is done to you.

Suppose we agree that there must be something better than our schools, something better suited to our human potential, our political ideals and our accelerating technology. What then? It is exactly at this point that there is a temptation to make what I believe is the basic educational blunder: Having tried and convicted the present educational system, one then works out in detail his own educational utopia—setting up a blueprint that covers matters such as curriculum, textbooks, administration policy, student-teacher ratio, classroom construction and so on.

From my point of view, however, a good school can't be described very clearly in advance because one essential characteristic of a good school is *the freedom to establish its own direction*. In fact, there may not even *be* such a thing as a good school within our present conception of what "school" means.

To say that learning is not something that is done to you has meaning on more than one level. With respect to the school as a whole, it means autonomy. There should be no dictatorial governing board or other body above the school making its decisions for it. If we are going to continue our policy of public education, this means that the people and their elected representatives will have to accept a new and radical policy: that they must pay for schools without controlling them. What happens, therefore, on a state university campus or on a junior high school campus would be decided neither by the legislature nor by the governor nor by any board of regents or board of education nor by any chancellor or superintendent of schools but only by the persons participating in the school itself. It is true that there would be a kind of power implicit in the fact that the state or community could refuse to pay for the school or could reduce its funds. But that would be the limit. To the extent that a state or city wanted to have a school, it would have to pay for it and leave it alone. Hopefully, the idea of an externally controlled school will in time become a contradiction in terms.

Autonomy in schools would almost certainly create much greater diversity—something that should be very good for us as individuals and as a society. As it is, almost all of our schools, at any given level, are amazingly alike. Given the way they are governed, this is not surprising. But what if schools were autonomous? Naturally there would be standardizing forces. The overall needs of society—the proliferating communications networks—a considerable degree of cultural cohesion—these would tend to restrain diversity in schools. But still, if schools were autonomous, they would show much more variety than they do now. Schooling arrangements in a given neighborhood would more closely reflect the character of the neighborhood. The country's colleges would offer a much wider and more interesting choice. There would be more experimentation and consequently a greater opportunity for one school to learn from the varied experiences of others. Schools might, in fact, begin to look more like a free enterprise system—but an educational rather than an economic one (free enterprise has always made much more sense to me in connection with the production of ideas than with the production of automobiles).

Also, if schools were autonomous, I would expect our rigid system of educational levels to weaken. There might well be large centers where persons of all ages would learn from each other and where the structural divisions would be based on areas of learning rather than on age. School might emerge less as a molding and screening process that usurps the first third of a person's life than as a continuing opportunity for certain kinds of learning and group activity.

Ideas about curriculum would also become much less rigid, since curriculum would be determined not by centralized authority but by the learners' and teachers' own awareness of what is relevant and necessary to

them and their society. On one campus you might find
a curriculum in light; on another a school of ecstatic
pharmacology. Radical movements would develop
through schools, not against them. The departmental
concept would probably fade. The concept of "curriculum" itself would perhaps become dated.

It's not my intention to predict everything that would
result from autonomy in schools. My basic point is
simply that autonomy is necessary if we want schools
to become places where you can learn without being
deadened and intimidated in the process and where
adaptive social change is fostered rather than prevented.

To say that learning is not something that is done to
you implies the need for more than just autonomy.
Within the school it means that everyone must have a
voice in the decisions that affect him. This kind of
arrangement—democracy—doesn't eliminate discord
but it does put the responsibility for a school on all of
the people in it.

I can't see any reason why either students or teachers
should be shut out of the decision-making process. In
fact, the supposed conflict between students and teachers
doesn't itself seem to be a basic one; it arises rather
out of the coercive and judgmental powers that have
been held by teachers and out of the slave role that
has been forced on students. In an autonomous and
noncoercive school, I would expect most disagreements
to cut across this tenuous boundary in other directions.

I hesitate to go on about students and teachers. The
very categories need to be questioned. The most meaningful distinction may be no more than an economic
one: who gets paid for what he does? And when we
all get paid for what we do, that distinction will disappear. Suppose that today I teach gymnastics, tomor-
row I study Arabic and the next day I participate in
an encounter group. In which category do I belong?

Administrator is still another term. Right now it's in
bad repute with many of us because administrators are
there to do the bidding of some external authority. In

an autonomous and democratic school, *administration* would just be people running their own school. A high school administrator for example, could be either a student or a teacher; he would be more or less a blackboard monitor on a somewhat larger scale. But this category also would be blurred at the very least.

To prevent education from being victimization, it will not be enough to have autonomy and democracy for the school as a whole. One would also want individual groups within a school to be free to develop their own learning structures without being pushed around and standardized by some central administration. However, I want to avoid falling into the trap I described earlier; I want to avoid trying to blueprint an educational utopia in advance. Self-government in practice cannot help but fall short of an ideal and therefore admits of endless approaches. If schools can serve as workshops in self-government, it will be both likely and valuable that they be diverse in this respect.

If schools are free, some of them may choose to renounce a part of their freedom. There may be students who prefer to be dictated to. For all I know there may always be students who want to be graded daily and threatened with probation, dismissal and so on, just as there may always be persons who want to be flogged and will no doubt always find other persons willing to do it. It is certainly not my wish to prevent them.

The freedom I talk about, incidentally, is not merely a matter of "academic" freedom. Schools are not just learning places but communities as well. Many schools are communities in the full sense of the word: people don't just go to them; they live in them. And, in the future, the distinction between "school" and "community" is likely to be much vaguer than it is now. Rochdale, for example, in Toronto, may be a sign of what is to come.

Rochdale is a number of things. To begin with, it's a new 18-story building. The people who live and pay rent in it own it and run it. For some of them it's a very loosely structured place to learn—a sort of experimental college. For others it's just a place to live. There are, furthermore, people who participate in educational activities of Rochdale but who don't live there. Rochdale is also a continuing problem—a place where there is no one to blame things on, where people have to improvise their own structures and to decide what to do with their freedom. Here is a paragraph, titled "The Secret," from one of their pamphlets:

> The secret of dealing with the confusion and uncertainty of Rochdale is to use "we" in place of "they" when referring to the operations of the College. For example, say "what we are going to do with the 17th floor terrace" rather than "what are they going to do, etc." This simple trick clarifies many otherwise ambiguous problems and helps eliminate flatulence.

I hope Rochdale thrives. And even more I hope the idea spreads.*

(8) "THE POWER TO SAY 'NO'"

The people who control colleges are fond of pointing out to students that higher education is a privilege. The implication is that if they don't behave, the privilege will be withdrawn. Similarly, in high school the ultimate threat is expulsion. School is supposed to be some kind of favor that society grants you. The condition for continuing to receive this favor is that you accept it on society's terms.

Sweat shop owners used to tell their workers more or less the same thing. It's astonishing that workers swallowed that line for so long. And it's equally as-

---

* If you're interested in free schools, you ought to read a beautiful essay by Dennis Lee, "Getting To Rochdale," in "The University Game" (Toronto, 1968). The essay originally appeared in "This Magazine is about Schools" (Winter, 1968).

tonishing that most students continue to see schooling as a privilege rather than as a transaction in which they happen to be getting a rotten deal.

When you go to school, you do society an enormous favor; you give it the opportunity to mold you in its image, stunting and deadening you in the process. What you get in return is access to a certain income bracket and the material comforts that go with it. But think what you've given up. Other animals have much of their nature born in them. But you were born with the freedom to learn, to change, to transcend yourself, to create your life—that's your human birthright. In school you sell it very cheap.

I have already tried (in Notes 3 and 4) to show that this rotten bargain isn't even good for society, that it forestalls necessary social change. Unfortunately, the dying part of society, which controls schooling, is also the part least likely to understand the need for profound change. It is the students—the not entirely socialized—who most feel the need for change and who, in trying to transform the society in which they live, become the victims of its self-protective rage.

The power that students have is simply the power not to be students, to refuse a bad bargain, as workers have frequently done—to say "no." If students have power, it is because they have something society needs very badly. Student power is made possible by the dying society's need to remain alive—to preserve itself through its children. Think how our institutions feed on the unformed future. Think even how individuals—those aging businessmen on a college board of trustees —clutch at immortality by putting their trip on the young. Society *needs* students to retain its identity; they are the only future it has. For this reason, students can demand freedom from exploitation and can get that freedom. They can insist that the continuity they provide society be one that is achieved through rebirth rather than through petrification.

There are a multitude of approaches that students can take toward changing schools. But the one that offers the most hope is the strike or boycott. It is more than a gesture, more than a pressure tactic. It cuts right to the heart of the problem. It refuses a bad bargain; it puts the future on strike. Requests can be denied or put off. Demonstrations can be broken up and the protesters put in jail. But a strike is not really vulnerable to force. When Governor Reagan of California recently promised to keep San Francisco State College open at the point of a bayonet if need be, he failed to understand both the limitations of the bayonet and the power of the student revolution.

High school students are in a more difficult position but this has not stopped them from beginning to use boycotts as well as other forms of noncooperation in order to change their schools. A few high school troublemakers can be expelled or disciplined in other ways. But what does it mean to expel most of the students in a school—especially when you've already compelled them to be there? Also, because these students are so regimented and because they are actually compelled to attend, a high school strike, though very difficult to bring about, is an even more dramatic and powerful action than is a college strike.

I have not yet said anything about the possibility of faculty-student cooperation in changing the nature of school. Such cooperation is difficult; most faculty members are still very much caught up in their roles and, even though they have their own reasons to want to change things, are reluctant to make common cause with students. Faculty, furthermore, are very hesitant to engage in the kind of forceful actions that might endanger their jobs or even their chances for promotion, tenure and so on. Still, there are enough instances of student-faculty cooperation to keep this an important possibility even at present. In order, though, for such cooperation to advance rather than impede student progress, it is essential that students don't wait around for faculty support and that they don't allow professorial timidity to rub off on them.

The American Federation of Teachers represents a

relatively militant segment of faculty; they have shown themselves, at San Francisco State in particular, to be a possible ally for the student movement. But it must be remembered that the AFT chose to join the students in striking at S.F. State in great part because it was an excellent opportunity to push their own drive for collective bargaining. AFT militancy—to the extent that they possess it—is directed toward rather limited goals. It would be a mistake to assume that the majority of AFT members, in high school or college, are stalwart supporters of the student liberation movement or even that they understand it.

In the long run, if students and teachers can outgrow their feudal relationship, they do indeed have a common cause: the freeing of schools from domination by outside forces. Perhaps the best thing students can do with respect to faculty is, first of all, to emphasize that common cause and to fully support faculty moves for greater self determination and, second, to work ceaselessly to educate teachers, to show them what's lacking in school as it is and to show them what education could be.

THE FOUR-FOLD PATH TO
STUDENT LIBERATION

THE WAY OF DIRECT ACTION

The basic method of direct action, as it has developed on campus, is simple. You organize, demand and negotiate; if negotiations break down, you work up (or stumble on) appropriate action projects in order to break through the impasse or at least to apply pressure for change. Meanwhile, you seek the widest possible campus and community support.

When students go into direct action, faculty and administrators frequently protest that such methods have no place in an institution of learning. They argue that the very nature of a college requires that disagreements be resolved by the use of reason, not coercion. This argument might have more weight if you, the student, got to define what is reasonable and if the whole college structure weren't, in fact, based on coercion.

The group that gets direct action going needn't itself be large but it must be capable of winning strong student support. This question of student support is a difficult one to deal with. On the one hand, if you postpone acting until you know that the majority of students are with you, you may never act at all. But, on the other hand, if your actions don't bring you support, if you don't keep winning students over, then you can't hope for anything but what the school administration is kind enough to give you. I emphasize this because the scope of a group's demands and of its actions should depend in part upon what it can expect from the student body. On some very enlightened cam-

47

pus, for example, where the students are really together, an action group might be ready to demand that the campus be turned over entirely to the students and faculty to run as they see fit, and it might want to support that demand with a strike—a total shutdown. On some other campus, however, the group might find itself hung up picketing to extend library hours. The student movement is full of surprises, though. Stupid, iron-fisted tactics by administrators can transform a very sleepy campus into a hot spot.

In setting up demands it's usually best to go after changes in the decision-making process whenever possible. Student liberation becomes more likely as students stop asking for handouts and begin instead to demand a piece of the action. It's more meaningful to insist on full participation in curriculum decisions than to push for a particular course or major. And, while it's worthwhile to protest the firing of a good teacher, you know that even if that particular teacher is rehired, there will probably be another such firing before long. What students ought to go after is involvement in decisions about hiring and firing. At Simon Fraser University in Vancouver, for example, a number of departments have students on committees that make personnel decisions; one large department has equal student representation in every area; that is, it is run jointly by students and faculty. Incidentally, students at Simon Fraser show no signs of being content with partial liberation. Last fall 114 of them went to jail for a demonstration demanding changes in admissions policy and the extension of student involvement in that area of decision making.

Administrators are often willing to *give* what students ask for as long as everyone understands that it is in fact a gift and as long as the hierarchy is maintained. But what they don't want to do is move over and let the students in—what the administrators, chancellors, trustees and legislatures absolutely do not want to do is surrender power. "Students," they say, "aren't competent to make academic decisions." "Students are only here four years; we abide forever." "We are not responsible to the students but to the taxpayers" (or trustees or archdiocese or whatever). There are always endless reasons not to give up power. Just the same, if there's going to be student liberation, then the position of slavemaster has got to go. It's not that "power" is the answer to all of students' problems. But as long as schools are run by someone else, students will continue to be victims rather than learners; education will continue to be something which is *done to* students. "Student power" isn't a false label, just an inadequate one; "student self-determination" and "student liberation" are closer to the heart of it.

In any case, after you've worked out your demands, let's say that you go up to the highest-ranking administrator and lay them on him. Naturally, if he's obstinate and remains so, you'll have to consider some kind of action project. But what if he isn't? What do you do if the administrator is really a pleasant accommodating person? Suppose, as he sends out for coffee and sandwiches, that he tells you how significant your proposals are. Suppose he takes you behind the scenes, where decisions are made, and shows you what the limitations of his position are. Suppose he sets up a committee to study your suggestions. Maybe he even gives you a little of what you asked for. Just a taste so you don't go away empty-handed. With an administrator like this, you have to be very strong indeed, very certain of your goals, and very well prepared and organized. When he asks what specifically you want him to do, you must be able to tell him. If it's the authorities above him that turn out to be the obstacle, then you need to make it clear that you will carry the campaign to them. Above all, it's essential to retain your radical goals as well as your readiness to engage in direct action. You have to be very resistant to top-management rhetoric and razzle-dazzle. Otherwise you'll dissolve in his affability and never be heard from again.

If you insist that administrators play the role of villain, you are likely to be led into some great foolish-

ness. However, if you flatly accept their methods, their
style and their formulation of the problem, then you
have almost certainly copped out. Of course, should
the administrator himself happen to be a real educational radical, then you need to work with him in
dealing with the more conservative forces that undoubtedly beset him. But this is not too likely. More probably
he is an educational liberal who would like to keep
all parties content without having to make any dizzy-
ing changes. "It is the genius of administration," Paul
Goodman has written, "to enforce a false harmony in
a situation that should be rife with conflict." Can you
dig it?

Suppose, though, that you run into a more old-fash-
ioned model of administrator. He tells you more or
less to go fuck yourself and threatens to suspend the
lot of you. In this case, you've lucked out. You've got
the administration working for you.

So you start the ditto machines going and you get
into some direct action, escalating as necessary and as
you gain strength. There's usually no point in doing
more than you have to. At L.A. State, several years
ago, the students won on a particular issue simply by
picketing the administration building for a month and
then threatening to picket and boycott the new president's inauguration (these students did, it should be
added, have considerable faculty support). And I know
of a junior high school where the principal forbad possession of the local underground newspaper. A few
days later, over a hundred students showed up con-
spicuously carrying the paper; that was all they had
to do. But if you're after something big—or if you have
a really pigheaded administration—then it won't go that
easy.

There's not much point in going over here the various
kinds of direct action that have appeared in the last
ten years. As a matter of fact, it's usually best to try
to create your own. Say, for example, that over the last
six months, students have been occupying buildings on
campuses across the country. You could do the same

on your campus. But there's a kind of diminishing return involved. The impact decreases and the ability of administrators to cope with the action increases. Better either to try to improve on the action or else to come up with something entirely different. Perhaps, instead of camping in one building, you devise roving actions that stay one step ahead of the police.

For students, the most powerful of all direct actions is probably a strike. It may well become as important to them as it has been to the labor movement. A student strike puts extremely heavy pressure on the administration (you just can't administer a school for long without students); it is also much harder to counter than a sit-in. A strike, however, demands a considerable degree of support at the outset. It needn't have majority participation at first but if a strike doesn't begin with more than a small band of campus radicals, it isn't too likely to thrive.

The road to a strike, unfortunately, often seems to lead through jail. That is, a relatively small number of students engage in some kind of militant confrontation; then they get busted; then other students begin to become aware of what's happening. The strike finally develops mainly as a protest against the administration's repressive tactics. Thus far, students have generally been reluctant to strike simply to achieve educational reform; they do it to protest mass arrests or suspensions, to protest police on campus and so on. The original demands, of course, are always thrown in with the package but the real impulse seems to come as a reaction to jailing, bloodshed and other heavy repression. This is a problem that emphasizes the importance of trying to educate other students, no matter how frustrating the task may seem. As they come to understand what goes on in school; as their educational goals become more far-reaching and radical, and as they realize their own potential power, then they will become more willing to strike without any preliminary massacres to urge them on.

Striking may be the most effective form of noncooperation on campus but it is far from the only one. A less ambitious but still powerful kind of direct action can consist simply of refusing to follow stupid orders. A rally, for example, is direct action if rallies have been banned (such a ban was recently declared on the San Fernando Valley State College campus; the next day well over two hundred students and community supporters held a rally and were arrested). In a high school with a code of dress it might be a good direct action if a substantial number of students would just attend barefoot or in some other "illegal" way. And I know of several colleges where students have invaded the faculty lounge or faculty cafeteria. In one of those colleges, the faculty cafeteria was permanently opened to students as a result. Another possibility is boycotting a particularly bad course or even department. And noncooperation is also an excellent way to deal with censorship of publications. Just do everything possible to print what you want regardless of the censor. If you lose your job, you can start an underground publication on campus. If you get kicked out of school, this may stir students to action. Fuck censorship. A toy newspaper on campus is probably worse than none at all.

Sometimes student direct actions are not planned at all. There's a rally. It ends up at the administration building. Someone orders the crowd to leave. They refuse. Zap. You're in the middle of a sit-in.

Occasionally these actions are not as spontaneous as they look. But often, the students who thought they were running a rally are surprised by the direction it takes. And then they get into a flurry of whispered conversations about whether what is going on is good tactics or not. Friendly faculty members, while supporting the principle involved, often come up with a dozen reasons why the timing is bad and why the demonstration should be put off. My own experience with unplanned demonstrations on and off campus has been fairly good. One that I remember closed the Los Angeles Federal Building at the time of the Selma march. The "official" groups initiating it didn't like the way it was going and pulled out. So those of us who remained there improvised our own direct action. And when the apparent leaders were arrested in mass bust, new leaders arose to take over. There are always plenty of reasons to be found for postponing a strong, arrestable direct action. But if the enthusiasm and the willingness are there, it's a shame to get in their way.

If you choose the way of direct action, there is always a great danger of selling out early in the game for a few trivial concessions. You come away with the appearance of victory; you hold a big celebration, but things stay pretty much as they were before. There is one particular form that this danger commonly takes: Demonstrators are arrested on campus and perhaps suspended. Then there is an outcry; students demand that the demonstrators be reinstated and that the charges be dropped. This itself then becomes the issue, rather than the demands over which the original demonstration took place. Eventually some sort of compromise may be reached in which the students halt their action program in return for the demonstrators' amnesty. The victory is a phony one. You end up exactly where you started.

Another danger in direct action is that the people involved will find themselves to be a small and isolated group of apparent fanatics with little or no support. This doesn't have to happen. If it does, it may mean that the action group is drastically out of touch with the student body it claims to represent. The group's members may be cliquish—reluctant to venture out of a small circle of sophisticates, where they take turns putting down their ignorant and apathetic fellow students. Or else it may mean that the educational issue has been so tightly welded to a particular form of political radicalism that all but a small number of students are shut out. I don't think that a person who is radical both educationally and politically should hide either conviction or should pretend to be anything but what he is. But there is some advantage in keeping even a slight distinction between the two areas. Student liberation is a worldwide movement and an issue that cuts across political and social divisions. Berkeley's FSM, for example, included representatives of both the right and the left. This doesn't mean that a political radical loses his identity in an educational movement—only that he accepts the possibility of cooperating in certain limited contexts with students whose politics are other than his.

Still, this matter is almost hopelessly complicated. The problems exploding on campus, as is pointed out almost daily by someone or other, are the problems of society at large. And though the educational issue may become more distinct in time, right now it usually shows up, in direct action, tied to the issue either of racism or of war. Last year a number of us—students and teachers—were arrested in a demonstration opposing Dow Chemical recruitment at L.A. State. It was, obviously, an anti-war action. It was also participated in by Third World representatives, including the Black Students Union, as a move against racist imperialism. And it was also regarded by many students as a student-power protest against the administration's unilaterally established placement policy. The strikes at S.F. State and Berkeley, the widely publicized student occupation at Columbia, as well as student actions in Mexico, France and other countries all show a blending of educational issues with other issues. Still, the worldwide student movement has an identity of its own which can be *somewhat* distinguished from racial, political and economic movements. It is the revolt of an exploited population—an exploited class, if I can use the term very loosely. And this exploited class exists anywhere in the world where education is something *done to* students—in the name of no matter what system, ideology or national ideal.

I have mentioned some dangers that attend student direct action. There is one that is quite serious though it has so far been resisted for the most part. That danger is the temptation to use violence as direct action—by violence I mean physical assault on other people. The mass media, not surprisingly, enormously inflate the role of violence in student action.* Generally, "VIOLENCE

---

* The grotesquely disproportionate emphasis on student violence can't be blamed entirely on the press. People tend to be indulgent toward police violence—to discount it. This remains true even when the journalists themselves are beaten by cops. A *San Francisco Chronicle* reporter, for example, was attacked by police while covering the S.F. State conflict. The man, John Leaning, had his press ID in full view on his jacket but it did him no good; a policeman smashed him in the face, beat him to the ground and then kicked him in the kidneys. In the paddy wagon he saw four plainclothes cops force a man to lie on the floor while they beat him on the base of the spine with their clubs. The *Chronicle* printed this story on January 19, 1969 but so what? Throughout California the public outcry is still directed almost entirely against students; the police remain heroes and protectors.

The press both feeds and reflects public fears: fear of change, fear for the prerogatives of race, age and property, and also the deep fear that people have of anyone that they have exploited and subjugated. People tend to see police violence in small scale, as though through the wrong end of a telescope, while every instance of violence by students is magnified tenfold.

Leaning's experience, furthermore, is relatively minor. More and more often now students are victims of "law enforcement" so bloody, so sadistic as to encourage one's worst fears not just about police but about human beings in general. But the smug bastards on television call for sterner law enforcement. State legislators prepare hysterical statutes to crush "campus anarchy." It may be that the American people are becoming hardened to police violence and are learning to swallow their TV dinners while watching students being beaten with a brutality that would have horrified them ten years ago. And perhaps the hardening process is not yet complete. How long can people watch soldiers advancing on college students with full battle dress, gas masks and drawn bayonets, without beginning to assume that the bayonets and guns are there to be used?

It's all a TV show. No one seems to understand what's happening until his own skin is breached. Then he realizes what the black and brown ghettos have been trying to tell him all these years. You could see this realization exploding on people at the Century City nightmare in Los Angeles in 1967. For the thousands of middle-class caucasians who attended that peace march—many of them at their first demonstration—it was a four-year course in cops, condensed into one terrifying evening.

ON CAMPUS" turns out to mean that the cops have been cracking heads again. Sometimes though it is the cop's head that gets cracked when students throw bricks. Occasionally, striking students have beaten other students who crossed the picket line.

Violent direct action is a terrible mistake, I think, on two counts. First, it is usually a stupid tactic in campus situations; it strengthens the opposing forces enormously. Administration violence tends to build the student movement; student violence is a favor to the slave-master. But let's assume a situation where violence doesn't at all seem tactically stupid—it is still a mistake, though, from a point of view that looks beyond the narrow limits of one isolated time and place.

Violence perpetuates the ugliest and stupidest feature of human history. If we are ever going to get out of this bloody trap of violence and counter-violence, it will require that people begin to put it down *even in the face of violence from others and even in behalf of a* "*good cause.*" There are, of course, some who argue that we should remain violent just long enough to have one last revolution—whichever you choose—and that then we'll be able to give it up. I'm awed by their faith. Just one more violent revolution and then we're all supposed to get along fine. That idea is far more naively optimistic, I think, than expecting that the world will someday abandon violence. As a matter of fact, we need several kinds of revolution—and one of them has to be a revolution in the way we settle our differences. Without *that* one, without giving up the desecration of each other's bodies, all the other revolutions are likely to turn sour.

I'm not implying, by the way, that you or I have to run off and preach nonviolent resistance to the Bolivian guerrillas. We in this country are scarcely in a position to preach nonviolence elsewhere—especially to hungry Latin American peasants. Moreover, it may well seem to them that circumstances have locked them in to the cycle of violence. But we're not locked in. We're not the Bolivian guerrillas and there's no point playing at it like children who've just come out of a war movie. It's not so much oppressed peasants who need to learn about nonviolence; it's the United States, currently revealing itself as the most powerful and most violent country in the world. And we'll have to change this country in part by reducing its reverberating waves of violence not by increasing them. The U.S., as demonstrated by its actions, is a scary, power-mad, racist country. It will take more than political and economic change to straighten this country out. So Big John Wayne changes ideology. Say he even turns socialist. Don't you think he could still find reasons to turn his machine gun on the gooks or even on those hungry greasers to the south? I can dig socialism—but it's a large category and it does appear to contain *within* its confines ample room for revolution, war and even, Marx forbid, global disaster. To repeat: it's an illusion to assume that one more revolution will eliminate the basis of social and international discord; there's *always* a millenium around the corner. What we had better do is learn to change the way in which we manifest our discord.

You know, I've often noticed how infectious violence is. When the cops club you for the first time, you get all worked up like you just discovered something new. You start to think about bringing along your own club next time; you scream out "Fascist Pig!" with new fervor, and maybe you start explaining to people how nonviolence doesn't work after all. What's sad about this reaction, understandable though it may be, is that you've let the cops win—not because they've clubbed you or driven you off the street but because they have put their filthy trip on you. And when you turn violent, you just keep the trip going, to pass on to your children and grandchildren and all posterity . . . if there is any.

There is one other kind of direct action—destroying buildings and such like—that seems generally to be a great mistake (though it doesn't fall into my personal definition of violence). For one thing, there's often a serious danger that it could turn into violence, that it could injure or kill someone. But aside from that, it tends to turn people off in the same way that violence does. Still, I would rather see a building messed up than people. I would much much rather see a draft board burn than Asian peasants. Wouldn't you? However, such simple either-or situations rarely exist.

One further comment about direct action. It will not work very well where students have totally accepted their role as slaves. If that's what's happening on a campus, then the local troublemakers have a great deal to do before they can expect mass sit-ins and strikes. On such a campus it would be wise to spend time educating your fellow students, no matter how hopeless such a project seems. You could get speakers on campus; set up panels on educational reform; start an underground newspaper and an experimental college; develop a guerrilla theater group; put forth specific proposals to the administration as a way to develop and focus interest. And finally, on such a campus you would want to keep your ears wide open and find out where the students are and what bothers them. Trivial or not, it can be the thin end of the wedge.

Finally, it's worthwhile to consider the limitations of direct action. It is normally useful to move machinery around. It gets a law passed—eliminates a college rule —establishes a black studies major—gives students a voice in academic decisions. Direct action can force people to do something or to stop doing something. But it usually has drawbacks. Ordinarily, it emphasizes division and nourishes enmity; it keeps the game of *sides* going.

There is a kind of direct action that goes beyond division. What makes the difference is not so much the nature of the action as the attitude of the people doing it. If they themselves have gotten past playing cowboys and Indians—*us* and *them*—then the action, no matter how militant, may do more than simply move by force. It could be a sit-in, a strike, the occupation of a building. What gives it a power beyond coercion is the feeling of community behind it—not just community of "our side" but community of the whole.

Most of us, unfortunately, approach direct action with the spirit of rooters at a high school football game. This attitude itself reflects our competitive schools and our society, and it may be difficult to avoid at present. When you're in chains, you can't necessarily wait until your head is straight before trying to break them. But in the long run we're not going to be able to get rid of competitiveness and division with more of the same.

THE WAY OF THE PROVO

The way of direct action is easily explained. The way of the Provo is not. But let's start with this contrast: the typical direct action project is carried out to bring about some desired change. The Provo action *is* a desired change. A direct action may or may not be artful but it's always practical. A Provo action may or may not be practical but it's always aesthetic.

Let's say you picket for better coffee or to eliminate the grading system. That's the way of direct action. But suppose you set up a booth somewhere on campus and distribute a bushel or two of assorted green beans, artichokes, leeks and crookneck squash. Or suppose you paint all the toilet seats on campus. Or suppose you hold a charity drive, collecting canned goods to give to the various college deans. That's the way of the Provo.

Provo happenings can be as simple or as complex as you choose. You could create one with no more equipment than a piece of chalk or with as much as, say, two helicopters and several tons of rose petals. The Provo action on a campus improves it instantly. No waiting. It is true that some Provo actions have had an instrumental value but they have also been aesthetic. The original Amsterdam Provos, for example, left white bicycles lying around for people to take. This is practical because it helps to eliminate automobile traffic in the center of the city. But even if it didn't, it would still be a very pretty thing to do. The same point would apply if you blacked over the glass on all the clocks on campus. It would do a lot for the campus in more ways than one.

My friend, Peter, once suggested that it would be a very good thing if everyone brought children to campus one day. It certainly would. And if children are hard to find, how about water buffaloes?

Then there's cheating. Let's say you and a number of friends steal an advance copy of some multiple-choice test. If you use it to get high scores, that would be playing the same old game. But suppose everyone in the class were to make an exact 57? That would be something else again. You could do the same with term papers; everyone in a class could hand in a neatly typed copy of the same term paper.

.. Or how about decorating the campus? Start with a party in which you all cut out about five thousand pictures, preferably in color, from as assortment of nudist-camp magazines. Then you beautify the campus with them. Walls—blackboards—departmental bulletin boards. In library books. Stapled to the IBM cards. One in each school paper. Interleaved with tests to be passed out. Under the dishes of carrot salad in the cafeteria. Displayed in vending machine windows. Pussies and pricks all over, wherever you look. This would be a splendid happening for any place as far removed from the pubic realities as a college campus. Or, better yet, a high school campus. Incidentally, as a response to administration censorship of some supposed "obscenity," this idea might no longer be Provo but it would be a hell of a good direct action. I once tried to talk a Long Beach State student group into doing this after the chancellor had cancelled a master's-thesis art exhibit that was supposed to be obscene. I think that the group thought I was crazy. They chose to do the traditional thing and sat in a building instead. I still think they should have gone the picture route.

An L.A. Provo group went caroling in swank restaurants late in January. They also swept nine blocks of sidewalk once on the Sunset Strip. And they held a great smoke-in and street party on Fairfax Blvd., where they passed out two thousand numbers rolled out of marjoram, oregano, catnip and such like. Presumably some of the smoke-inners were smoking righteous dope but it would have been pretty hard for anyone to figure out which ones. Two men were arrested for possession but later cut loose when it was found they were smoking catnip.

There is, by the way, no point Provoing unless you really feel the urge—and if you really feel like it, you won't need to be supplied with ideas. Also, Provoing is *not* RFing. RF's are commonly done *to* somebody while Provo actions don't ordinarily need a target. Provo doesn't involve getting the best of people or screwing them up—but simply blowing their minds. Like if, when no one was around, you built a low brick wall across the middle of some classroom. Or what about big silent rallies? Silent discussion groups. *Silent days!*

Faculty have fine opportunities for Provoing, if they would just use them. I stumbled on one last year while trying to wiggle out of grading people in a poetry course. I swore I wasn't going to grade anybody any more on how they read poetry. On the other hand, both the students and the college insisted on grades. I could have just given all A's—but that would mean that the class would be filled up the next semester with people who only wanted to pick up the A, while many who really wanted to take the course would be turned away when it filled up. So I decided to grade but not to grade on poetry or on anything else that seemed to matter a great deal. The first test was on one day's programming in a TV guide. The midterm was on capital cities of the world. The final was on state flowers and governors.

The straightest teacher would make the best Provo. Take someone who's been walking in, reading his notes and walking out in every class for the last ten years. What if he walked in and silently started covering the blackboard with aerosol shaving cream in neat up-and-

down strokes? He would run out of stuff and would
have to go in his briefcase for another can. The whole
thing might take him 20 or 30 minutes. Magnificent!
Instant enlightenment for everyone in the class.

Provo happenings open up fresh possibilities in an
environment that's blurred with dullness and routine.
We are for the most part trapped under our own institutions, such as factories, prisons and schools. A
Provo happening helps to dig us out.

THE WAY OF THE SQUARE

When you work within the official structure and, as
ey say, "follow established channels," you go the way
of the square. On campus, that usually means participation in student government or in whatever administrative committees and so on have been opened up to
some student participation.

It's often a temptation to put this way down flat. But
you just can't. There are campuses where the only
progress toward student liberation is being made by
student government. Or where a few token student
members of faculty committees have managed to avoid
Tom-ing it up and have been able to confront faculty
and administration on a number of basic issues.

I'm not particularly optimistic about the possibility
of a student government actually liberating students
from external control. Perhaps the ideal student government would be a sort of suicide machine. It would
unilaterally grant students their freedom and would pro-
claim the school's autonomy. It would offer to confer
with the faculty to work out equitable approaches to
decision-making where both the students and faculty
are concerned. It would, of course, be promptly dis-
solved by the school authorities, who would point out
that they hold final responsibility for the administration
of the campus. The student government could then re-
constitute itself as a real student government—an
underground student government, if you like—aban-

doning the "official" puppet role. It would then be in a position to work for the students freely and without fear. It would also have helped to make the issues involved very clear.

Even a student government that falls short of this ideal can still do quite a bit for its constituency. If it maintains a constant heavy pressure for radical educational changes; if it refuses to be deceived by tokenism; if it supports those militant students who follow the way of direct action; if it insists on complete control of at least its own funds and activities; if it casts off the old slave trappings, the whole pompom-and-beanie mentality, and begins to act and spend money in meaningful ways; if it's willing to catch hell from the faculty, the administration, the alumni, some of its constituents and the community at large—then maybe a student government is worth supporting. It may even be worthwhile spending some time trying to elect this kind of student government. But I wouldn't hold my breath. What you're more likely to get is bigger Homecomings and maybe an extra wing on the student union, with more bowling alleys and pool tables to keep the children occupied.

Student government is not restricted to pressuring the administration for favors. It can utilize its own resources to achieve change. It can, for example, sponsor an experimental college. Experimental colleges put students in a better position to learn something while they're getting a degree. They do a lot to reduce the isolation and anonymity that a person feels attending a large college or university; in fact, many experimental colleges have groups with no other purpose than to bring students closer, often literally in touch, with each other and with themselves. The experimental college also offers a chance for people to learn what learning can be, to push past all the limitations and paralyzing assumptions that wreck "official" schooling, to push past even the very category of "school." And, by its freedom and its vitality, the experimental college is a continuing

criticism of the other, coercive college, whose students
it can help to liberate and educate.*

Several problems, though, have begun to appear in
connection with experimental colleges. One is that students tend to limit their experimenting to changes in
curriculum and the abolishment of grades. Uncertain
what to do with their freedom, they fall back upon
conventional approaches. This isn't a serious problem,
though; it's more of a transitional difficulty encountered
as people move from playing student to creating their
own education. Another problem has to do with the
advisability of going after academic credit for experimental college courses. Some persons, including myself,
feel that this seriously corrupts the function of an experimental college; for only when a course offers no
artificial inducement such as unit credit can all of its
participants be sure that they are there solely because
they really want to be there. Others argue, though, that
obtaining credit for its courses strengthens an experimental college and, furthermore, does much to improve
the "official" college. Incidentally, student government
itself can be a problem if it is not in sympathy with
the goals of an experimental college or if it gives itself
the right to censor or disapprove courses. Where there
is conflict of this kind, it is probably much better to
set up an experimental college entirely free of student
government.

It's hard to be too cautious about following the way
of the square. Just as some black radicals have been

---

* One such college, the Midpeninsula Free University, located at Palo Alto, has a course catalog as extensive as those
of many orthodox, non-experimental colleges. Among the
courses are Moonwatching, Underground Journalism, Egg Tem-
pera, Beginning Calculus, The Skies of Autumn, Witchcraft,
Toymaking, Urban Guerrilla Warfare and Communications En-
tropy. There are also over 50 encounter groups with titles such
as Here and Now, The Limits of Lesbos, Groove Experiential
and The Experience of Death. In addition, the MFU has gone
past the concept of courses; it sustains projects: a survival village, abortion counseling, a cooperative store, a legal defense
guild, and several others.

coopted by governmental structures, so educational radicals often find themselves drowning in the academic bureaucracy. Stupid administrators and student officials may persecute the radical. But bright ones put him on salary, pamper him and honestly may regard him as an unorthodox young go-getter with "a valuable contribution to make to the college community." The time may not be far away when educational revolutionaries will find themselves much more rewarded than persecuted, surrounded with small successes, encouraged even to play the role of rude and barefoot barbarian. They will help to usher in a New Deal period on campuses across the country. This may be some sort of progress but it will also be the very toughest (and hopefully last) line of defense for the slave-system in college. One of the worst things that could happen to the student movement is what happened to the labor movement: getting stuck halfway.

I don't mean to say that administrators who try to bring student radicals into the system are necessarily deceitful types. Quite the contrary, they are usually liberals with excellent intentions. Nor am I implying that it's *bad* for students to move into the very administrative openings that student demands have created. I simply want to point out the considerable danger of getting hung up part way to the goal. A recent TV documentary on Antioch College pointed out to viewers that the students, even when they are *given* (my emphasis) freedom, keep demanding more. Damn right they keep demanding more. It's as though Alabama passed a law giving half its black population the right to vote and then said, when the protests started, "You people are never satisfied." Getting stuck part way toward educational liberation comes from developing the kind of institutional involvement that dims your vision of what *ought* to be and drains your urgent need to get there now.

THE WAY OF THE SELF

Group action is not the only way to change a campus. Just being a person changes things. If you stop letting others define you; if you try to find out what you are and what you want; if you get yourself together, then you can't help but transform your environment. Colleges, for the most part, aren't set up to accommodate real people. They're tooled to process Ken and Barbie Dolls. If very many real people are fed into the machine, it will begin to break down. When people stop playing "student," they will be able to learn without surrendering themselves in exchange.

To be real in school is to be revolutionary because the school demands that you pretend to be something other than what you are. When you stop following the institutional script, the illusion fades and people start to look silly, strutting and posing and wearing those stupid masks. I've written in considerable detail in this essay about techniques for transforming school into something better and more human. Still, all of this is no more than a cumbersome footnote to one *in*sight, which cannot simply be transmitted like a key or a deed, but which, once you have hold of it, will never let you believe in "students" again. Even the phrase, "student liberation," may make you smile. We've always been free; all we need is to know it.

A YOUNG PERSON'S GUIDE TO
THE GRADING SYSTEM

There's no question that the grading system is effective in training people to do what they're told. The question is: what does it do for learning?

Grades focus our attention. But on what? On the test. Academic success, as everyone knows, is something that we measure not in knowledge but in grade points. What we get on the final is all-important; what we retain after the final is irrelevant. Grades don't make us want to enrich our minds; they make us want to please our teachers (or at least put them on). Grades are a game. When the term is over, you shuffle the deck and begin a new round. Who reads his textbooks after the grades are in? What's the point? It doesn't go on your score.

Oddly enough, many of us understand all of this and yet remain convinced that we need to be graded in order to learn. When we get to college, twelve years of slave work have very likely convinced us that learning is dull, plodding and unpalatable. We may think we need to be graded: we assume that without the grades we'd never go through all that misery voluntarily. But, in fact, we've been had. We've been prodded with phony motivations so long that we've become insensitive to the true ones. We're like those sleeping pill addicts who have reached the point where they need strong artificial inducement to do what comes naturally. We're grade junkies—convinced that we'd never learn without the A's and F's to keep us going. Grades have prevented us from growing up. No matter how old a person is—when he attends school, he's still a child, tempted with lollipops and threatened with spankings.

Learning happens when you *want* to know. Ask yourself: did you need grades to learn how to drive? To learn how to talk? To learn how to play chess—or play the guitar—or dance—or find your way around a new city? Yet these are things we do very well—much better than we handle that French or Spanish that we were graded on for years in high school. Some of us, though, are certain that, while we might learn to drive or play chess without grades, we still need them to force us to learn the things we don't really want to learn—math, for instance. But is that really true? If for any reason you really want or need some math—say, algebra—you can learn it without being graded. And if you don't want it and don't need it, you'll probably never get it straight, grades or not. Just because you pass a subject doesn't mean you've learned it. How much time did you spend on algebra and geometry in high school? Two years? How much do you remember? Or what about grammar? How much did all those years of force-fed grammar do for you? You learn to talk (without being graded) from the people around you, not from gerunds and modifiers. And as for writing—if you ever do learn to write well, you can bet your sweet ass it won't be predicate nominatives that teach you. Perhaps those subjects that we would never study without being graded are the very subjects that we lose hold of as soon as the last test is over.

Still, some of us maintain that we need grades to give us self-discipline. But do you want to see real self-discipline? Look at some kid working on his car all weekend long. His parents even have to drag him in for dinner. And yet, if that kid had been compelled to work on cars all his life and had been continually graded on it, then he'd swear up and down that he needed those grades to give him self-discipline.

It is only recently—and out of school—that I have begun to understand self-discipline in writing. It grows out of freedom, not out of coercion. Self-discipline isn't staying up all night to finish a term paper; that's slave work. Self-discipline is revising one paragraph fanatically for weeks—for no other reason than that you yourself aren't happy with it. Self-discipline is following a problem through tedious, repetitive laboratory experiments, because there's no other way of finding out what you want to know. Or it can be surfing all day long every single day for an entire summer until you are good at it. Self-discipline is nothing more than a certain way of pleasing yourself, and it is the last thing anyone is likely to learn for a grade.

Coercion inside school probably leads many of us to develop our self-discipline in areas untouched by the classroom. Who knows? If movie-going, dancing and surfing were the only required subjects, there might well be a poetic renaissance. I suspect that most kids fool around with writing on their own at some point—diaries, poetry, whatever—but this interest rarely survives school. When you learn that writing is intellectual slave work, it's all over.

Do you think you're a lazy student? No wonder! Slaves are almost always lazy.

Suppose I go to college; I want to be a chemist or a high school teacher or an accountant. Are grades really my only reason for learning the field? Is getting graded going to turn me on to my subject? Or is it more likely to turn me off? How sad this is. History is so engrossing. Literature is so beautiful. And school is likely to turn them dull or even ugly. Can you imagine what would happen if they graded you on sex? The race would die out.

Wouldn't it be great to be free to learn? Without penalties and threats, without having to play childish competitive games for gold and silver stars? Can you even imagine what the freedom to learn might be like?

Perhaps this kind of freedom sounds attractive to you but you're convinced that it isn't suited to our society. Even if the grading system can be shown to work against learning, you may assume that grades are still necessary to *evaluate* people—to screen people for various kinds of work.

But think about it. Do you really believe that the best way to determine someone's qualifications is to grade him—A, B, C, D, F,—week by week, day by day, in everything he studies for sixteen years of school? Is this monstrous rigmarole honestly necessary in order to determine who gets which jobs?*

There are far better ways to determine a person's qualifications. Many fields already do their own screening by examination; the bar exam is one instance. In some areas—journalism, for example—supervised on-the-job experience would probably be the most effective screening and qualifying technique. Other fields might call for a combination of methods. Engineers, for example, could be qualified through apprenticeship plus a demonstration of reasonable competency on exams at various levels—exams on which they would, of course, get an unlimited number of tries.

In a great many fields, no screening technique is necessary at all. Countless employers, public and private, require a college degree for no really good reason, simply because it enables their personnel departments to avoid making any meaningful individual evaluation and because it indicates some degree of standardization. There is no reason why a person should be forced to spend four years of his life in college just to get a

---

* In his article, "College Grades and Adult Accomplishment," published in "Educational Record" (Winter, 1966), Donald Hoyt reviews 46 studies dealing with the relationship between college grades and subsequent performance or "success." The studies cover a wide range of fields and use a variety of criteria for success. Among the fields in which a preponderance of studies has found no correlation between vocational success and undergraduate GPA are engineering, medicine, business, scientific research and teaching. In general, according to Hoyt, the various studies show either no correlation at all or, in some instances, "no more than a very modest correlation" between college records and adult success. Hoyt also comments, "The practice of basing admission to schools of education, business, engineering or medicine largely or exclusively on undergraduate grades seems indefensible."

decent job and then discover that he would have been much better off working in the field itself for four years and pursuing his own learning interests on a less rigid and formal basis.

Still it might be argued that eliminating grades entirely would require too sudden a shift in our society. I would maintain that the sudden shift is desirable. In any case, though, society is not likely to face the simultaneous abandonment of grading by every school in the country. Furthermore, on a campus where there is enormous resistance to abolishing grades, one could put forth a fairly good half-way compromise—the Credit system—which is, from my point of view, worth trying even though it falls short of what should be the real goal: no grades at all.

Under this system, some courses could be made totally free of grading: basic algebra, say, or drawing or poetry writing. The rest would be run on a Credit basis. If you meet the minimum requirements of a course, you get credit for it. No A's or C's or silver stars. Just credit. And if you don't meet the requirements, nothing happens. You don't lose anything or get penalized; you just don't get credit for that course. This is NOT the Pass-Fail System. Pass-Fail is a drag: if you don't pass a course, you get hurt. Under the Credit system you simply either get credit or you don't. All that your record shows is the courses you've earned credit for (not the ones you've attempted). And when you get credit for enough courses, you can get some kind of certification or credential, if you want one, according to the number and type of courses you've taken. And there should be not just a few assembly-line four-year degrees: AB, BS and so on; there should be scores of more meaningful and varied certifications and degrees. Or maybe there should be none at all, just a list of the courses for which you have credit.

What's wrong with that? College becomes something more like a place for learning and growth, not fear and anxiety. It becomes a learning community, not a gladiatorial arena where you're pitted in daily battle against your fellow students. In elementary and secondary schools, of course, there is an even weaker pretext for grading and even more to be gained by its abolishment.

And we mustn't be too quick to assume that abolishing A's and F's would make our colleges still more overcrowded. If we eliminate the pointless Mickey-Mouse requirements that are foisted on everyone, if we eliminate the gold-star games and all the administrative paperwork and class busywork that go along with them, if we reduce the overwhelming pressure for a meaningless, standardized degree, then perhaps we'll end up with learning facilities that can accommodate even more students than the number that get processed in the factories that we currently operate.

And if an employer wants not just degrees but grade-point averages too, the colleges will explain that that's not what they are there for. Graduate schools, for their part, will probably not present a serious problem. They already put heavy emphasis on criteria other than GPA's. They stress interviews, personal recommendations; most of them already give their own entrance exams anyway. Besides, the best graduate schools will probably be delighted to get some *live* students for a change.

But what about the students themselves? Can they live without grades? Can they learn without them? Perhaps we should be asking ourselves: can they really learn *with* them?

GORMAN

There were several taps at the door. Gorman finished printing "2nd QUIZ" at the top of a blue-lined column. He closed the record book and called out:

"Who is it?"

"Chuck Fernandez."

"From my eight o'clock?"

"Yes, sir."

"Just a sec. I'm on the phone."

Gorman moved quietly to a filing cabinet by the door. He eased open the top drawer a few inches and took out a revolver. Then, holding the revolver in his right hand, he stepped up on Ferguson's desk, which was next to the filing cabinet. From the desk he lifted himself on top of the cabinet and kneeled on its narrow summit, his head almost touching the ceiling. Turning his face away from the door, he called out:

"Come in."

The door flew open, slamming against the steel cabinet. Gorman peered down over the top of the door. It was Grunewald, of course. Grunewald's right hand was stuffed in his coat pocket; his head pivoted wildly from side to side as he scanned the empty room. He froze when he heard Gorman's voice coming from almost directly over his head.

"Don't move or I'll shoot you, Grunewald. Not the slightest move. Good. Now do exactly what I say. Take your empty right hand out of that coat pocket. Now reach your left hand in there and take that gun by the barrel. OK. Shut the door behind you with your right hand. All right, now hand the gun up to me. Thank you."

Gorman dropped Grunewald's pistol into his own left coat pocket; then he stepped down and sat on Ferguson's desk, watching the other man all the while.

"Take my chair and sit in it facing me."

Grunewald sat. "So I'm sitting. Congratulations. What are you going to do, shoot me, Gorman?"

Gorman was silent.

"Look, figure you picked yourself up a pistol on the deal. Goodbye. Good luck."

"Don't get out of that chair."

"Gorman, think! Plan ahead. Hold me here and you miss the meeting, too. What have you gained?"

"Don't worry about it, Grunewald. Now pick up my Trilling from the desk and read it—quietly."

"Shoot me, Gorman. I won't read Trilling."

Gorman reached into the open file drawer again, took out a silencer and began to fit it on his pistol. Grunewald, meanwhile, had located the Trilling. He began to read. It was quarter to three. The next fifteen minutes passed in silence punctuated by Grunewald's ostentatious sighs, snorts and tongue clickings. A minute or two after three there was another knock on the door. Gorman waited.

"Professor Gorman?"

He waited.

"Marshall, are you all right?"

"It's OK, Pam. Are any of Grunewald's people out there?"

"Yes, that clod, McGriff. Oh, and I passed Dr. Peaster in the hall but he's gone now."

Gorman whispered to Grunewald, motioning with the gun. "Tell McGriff to go away."

"McGriff, go away."

They heard McGriff call softly just outside the door: "Dr. Grunewald? Listen, if there's anything wrong . . ."

"McGriff, just go."

After a few moments Pam spoke from the corridor. "Marshall? He's gone."

"OK, come in."

She opened the door and shut it behind her as she looked at the two men. Without stepping between them, she walked over to Gorman and kissed him on the cheek.

"Ciao, Marshall. Hello, Dr. Grunewald. Marshall, aren't you going to your meeting? It's after three."

"That's all right. Look, I want you to stay here and watch Dr. Grunewald while I'm gone. When I leave, lock the door and don't open it till I get back. OK?"

"OK. Don't worry about it."

He gave her his revolver. "If he gets out of that chair, shoot him. Can you do it?"

"Shoot him! Oh, my God, Marshall. Ask me something difficult why don't you!"

"Pam." He looked at her for a moment. "We're voting on curriculum today."

She nodded soberly. "I'm sorry, hon. I'll be all right. Just take care of yourself."

"Sorority girls, Gorman?" Grunewald asked. "Are we going to see you at the prom?"

Pam leveled the gun icily. "I'm *not* in a sorority, Dr. Grunewald."

Gorman reached for his briefcase and opened the door. "Listen, Pam. McGriff or Professor Peaster or one of the others will be back. Make Grunewald send them away. Off campus somewhere. In the meantime, Grunewald, be quiet—and read."

He crossed the corridor into the men's room, patted his hair in front of the mirror and entered an empty stall, shutting and latching the door. He checked Grunewald's pistol to make sure that it was loaded. Then he put it in his right coat pocket. A swinging door had opened and shut. Gorman lowered his head below the top of the stall door.

"Marsh, it's Joel Peaster. I saw you come in. I'd like to talk to you for a minute."

"Just a minute, Peaster. I'm coming out." Gorman sank to his hands and knees and crawled silently under the partition into the next stall and then into the one beyond. One more partition brought him into the end stall. Its door was open a few inches, enough to reveal Peaster standing in front of the stall Gorman had been in. Peaster gripped a heavy glass ashtray in his right hand, which was poised at shoulder height. Gorman reached into his right coat pocket and spoke softly:

"Freeze, Peaster."

Several minutes later, his briefcase bulging with Peaster's clothes, Gorman raced up the escalator to the second-floor men's room. He dropped Peaster's underwear, shirt and tie in one toilet, his trousers in another and his coat in a third. He stepped on the flush pedal in each stall, then left the men's room and hurried down the corridor toward Lecture Hall 5. A few other latecomers were approaching the door. He entered with them and chose a seat on the aisle in the back row. About forty department members were already seated in front of him, scattered throughout the descending rows of padded, permanent seats.

They were winding up Old Business: allocation of out-of-state travel funds. When it was done, Gorman rose and introduced a motion to eliminate the second semester of the two-semester literary criticism requirement, and to substitute for it a required senior course in Chaucer. As Gorman stated his motion, the chairman, Wainwright, was scanning the rows of seats intently. When Gorman concluded, the chairman left his rostrum and walked over to the side wall where Roger, the departmental clerk, was standing. He spoke with the clerk briefly and then returned to the rostrum and addressed Gorman.

"Marshall, I wonder if you'd mind holding off on that motion for a few minutes. I notice that we're still missing several department members who have expressed particular interest in curriculum matters. Joel Peaster, for example, and Sid Grunewald . . ."

Wainwright was interrupted by shouts from the floor. Someone called out, "That's their problem!" A number of others, however, agreed with the chairman. Gorman spoke out over the hubbub.

"As a matter of fact, neither Professor Peaster nor Professor Grunewald will be able to attend at all. They both asked me to relay their apologies."

The shouted remarks from the floor, as well as a number of whispered conversations, continued. When they had subsided slightly, Gorman, still standing, reintroduced his motion to substitute Chaucer for second-semester Criticism. The chairman, Wainwright, however, ruled Gorman's motion out of order on the grounds that proper written notice had not been given 10 days in advance. Gorman appealed this ruling of the chair; from his briefcase he produced and distributed Xeroxed copies of an affidavit from Donna, the departmental secretary, affirming that a notice of intent had been placed in each professor's box two weeks previously. Nevertheless, Gorman's appeal, though it won a majority vote, narrowly missed obtaining the necessary two-thirds' approval.

Gorman waited. A few minutes later he found an opportunity to reintroduce his motion as an amendment. Van Pelt had moved to add a new lower-division requirement: Great Issues in Criticism. Gorman's amendment stipulated that no more than one semester of criticism be required for the major, and it added as requirements a senior course in Chaucer and a lower-division survey of Middle English poetry. Before Gorman had completed his amendment, there were a number of shouts of "Point of order!" Wainwright quieted the meeting and ruled Gorman's amendment out of order on the grounds that its thrust ran counter to the thrust of the Van Pelt motion.

At this point, however, Ronceval, the parliamentarian, slipped his right hand into a coat pocket which was already heavily weighted and sagging, and slouched from his seat in front to converse with Wainwright behind the rostrum. He stood partially behind Wainwright and whispered in his left ear. Wainwright listened to Ronceval for a minute or so. Then he addressed the meeting:

"I have decided, on advice of the parliamentarian,

to reverse my own ruling. Professor Gorman's amendment, which would limit our criticism requirements to
one semester and would add required courses in Chaucer
and Middle English poetry, is a proper amendment and
may stand. Is there any debate on the amendment?"

"What do you mean debate?" Van Pelt was on his
feet, shouting. "That's not an amendment. It's sabotage!
What is this?"

Wainwright spoke, almost whispering. "Stanley, I
have ruled it a proper amendment." Wainwright's glance
slid to the far left corners of his eyes, then rolled back
to focus intently on Van Pelt. "I hope you can understand my position."

"You're damn right I understand your position. Tell
Ronceval to get his hand out of his pocket."

There was an outbreak of murmuring and whispered
discussion. Ronceval remained where he was standing.
The chair called again for debate on Gorman's amendment.

Three speakers on each side had been heard and
Wainwright had already asked for ayes when Schlemmer rose and requested a secret ballot. Gorman stood
up in opposition, pointing out that the vote was already
in progress; he called for a ruling from the chair. Ronceval, who was still standing behind Wainwright,
whispered a few words in the chairman's ear. Wainwright ruled in Gorman's favor. There were a number
of calls for the parliamentarian to sit down and to take
his hand out of his coat pocket. Then Roger, the departmental clerk, who had moved over against the back
wall of the lecture hall, plunged his own right hand
into his own sagging coat pocket and moved swiftly up
behind Ronceval, where he whispered something in the
parliamentarian's ear. Ronceval listened for a moment,
then slowly raised his hands in a theatrical yawn and
let them come to rest casually behind his head, where
they remained. Elbows up, back arched, apparently
frozen in mid-yawn, Ronceval in turn whispered to
Wainwright, who promptly announced that he was re-
versing his ruling and would allow a secret ballot after

all. He called for Van Pelt and Schlemmer to count
ballots.

Schlemmer, however, announced, after a brief whispered exchange with Gorman, who was seated behind
him, that one of his contact lenses had popped out,
rendering him incapable of counting ballots. He insisted
that Gorman take his place.

Someone called out, "Schlemmer, what is this? Since
when . . ." He was interrupted by Van Pelt, who was
racing up the aisle toward Schlemmer. Van Pelt ran
awkwardly. His right hand was stuffed in his coat pocket and his left was waving above his head, with the
thumb and forefinger pressed together at the fingertips
making a circle. He shouted:

"I've found your lens, Schlemmer. Get moving. Never
mind Gorman."

However, Gorman had already sprinted down to the
rostrum and had taken a position behind Roger, the
departmental clerk. He whispered to the clerk, who
jerked promptly and convulsively into Ronceval's fro-
zen-yawn position and walked, elbows still in the air,
back to the side wall. Ronceval, in turn, dropped his
arms and whispered to Wainwright.

Wainwright announced that Gorman and Ferguson
would count ballots. Donna, the departmental secretary,
prepared the ballots and was distributing them when
one of the doors to the corridor burst open and Grunewald entered. He apologized for his tardiness, conferred
briefly and softly with Van Pelt and took a seat in the
back row. A minute or two later, after the ballots had
been handed out, Grunewald lurched to his feet and
clawed at the air, shrieking unintelligibly. After a moment, he fell back against the wall, stared blankly at
his colleagues, mumbled, "It's my heart" in a cracked
whisper and pitched forward over the row of seats in
front of him. The department members remained im-
mobilized, all but Gorman, who was at Grunewald's
side in an instant. He bent over Grunewald briefly,
then looked up and spoke:

"He's all right, actually. Call for the question."

At this point a number of things happened.

Grunewald, still collapsed over the seats, screamed, "What the hell do you mean all right? I'm dying here. Stop the meeting!" Then an explosion reverberated in the lecture hall, followed after a momentary hush by perhaps a dozen more, as faculty members scrambled in various directions over the seats and through the aisles. Van Pelt, his right hand bloody, scooped up a pistol from the floor with his left and dived behind the rostrum, shouting "Second-semester criticism, *over here!*" Ferguson and Fowler were standing toe to toe in the fourth row, battering each other in the face and head with briefcases. Peaster, who had been absent from the meeting, appeared striding down the right aisle, barefoot, in cap and gown, and bellowing, "Where IS that son of a bitch?" Gorman meanwhile was crouched in the last row of seats, Grunewald's pistol in his hand. Schlemmer was sprawled face down near the rostrum, as were Ronceval and Roger, the departmental clerk. Grunewald, holding Gorman's gun with the silencer attached, stood in the doorway, screaming "McGriff! McGriff!"

TEACHING JOHNNY TO WALK:

AN AMBULATION INSTRUCTION PROGRAM FOR THE NORMAL PRESCHOOL CHILD

(Note: This particular satire on schooling is dedicated to those who have nauseated themselves on a surfeit of academic journal articles. Others—lacking such rigorous training—may find it impossible to read.)

I. THE PROBLEM

A search of the literature pertaining to preschool education reveals scant recent investigation in the field of ambulation insofar as it is conceived in terms of the normal child. Certain related problems have, of course, been dealt with more extensively, e.g., the exceptional child, *vide* Cervelle (1) and Rolando (2) on brain damage; Ford (3) on autism, and my own work (4,5, 6) on the effects of ambulation motivation argumentation in cases of spatial disadvantaging occurring as a concomitant to traumatic peer-group deprivation, work which, of course, owes heavily to Guhl's pioneering and controversial "closest-children" experiments (7). Nevertheless, despite undeniable accomplishments in teaching the underachiever to walk, normal ambulation learning has received short shrift from specialists and has for the most part been left to the catch-as-catch-can empiricism of the family milieu, a milieu which fosters what one researcher (8) has termed "the invariable 'come to daddy' technique of the nonspecialist."

The time becomes increasingly propitious for the formulation of a viable theoretical basis for ambulation instruction on the normal preschool level. In the pilot study to be described, this writer and his associates sought to introduce into this hitherto unprobed area a variety of techniques drawn from recent literature on other preschool learning situations. The two principal techniques upon which our ambulation instruction program relies are Richardson's and Chambers' *life milieu deprivation* (9) and Kalstadt's *rehearsal prolongation* (10).

II. THE PILOT STUDY

A. LIFE MILIEU DEPRIVATION

Forty preambulatory nonexceptional preschoolers were institutionalized and discouraged from all spontaneous and voluntary attempts at ambulation. To reduce the subjects' ambulation attempt level, a variety of inhibitory techniques were applied, including the following:

1. the multi-wheeled "Crazy Shoe," developed by Shute (11) in his work on frustration tolerance;
2. Damper's (12) discouragement response symbols;
3. Gouneigh's (13) Nonsense Tapes (in which the operational message was "good children lie flat");
4. the Tele-Algic Teaching Control Wand, successfully utilized by De Lorres (14) to raise control levels in the inner-city classroom;
5. radical ceiling abasement (15).

The inhibitory system functioned at optimum levels throughout the pilot study (which is still in operation—this will be explained below). In fact, one unforeseen but beneficial result of the inhibitory system was the subjects' rapid value introjection, to the point that on one occasion several subjects joined in physically aggressive behavior unmistakably intended to inhibit the ambulatory attempts of a subject who had been introduced later than his peers into the experimental environment and who was removed from the pilot study shortly afterward for hospitalization. Thus the inhibitory set functioned as an unanticipated orthogonal, inducing persisters and achievers among the subjects toward self-activated participation in an interpersonally rich learning environment.

B. REHEARSAL PROLONGATION

1. *The Kinetic Schema*

As soon as the inhibitory system had reduced ambulation attempts to a negligible level, we began the first of various operations which together constitute the rehearsal prolongation system.

In preparation, we had carried out a kinetic analysis of normal ambulation samples and had created a kinetic schema based on the ten phases of ambulation diagrammed in Figs. A-J. This schema, although admittedly a distorted one, does provide the child with a structured learning situation. Furthermore, it allows for the maximum ambulatory standardization possible on a preschool level.

The rehearsal system began with a concentration on phase (b) dextral thrust—suprapatellar. The phase was, of course, rehearsed by our subjects in a supine rather than an upright position. Supine rehearsal helped to insure an acceptable Richardson level of life milieu deprivation; it also better enabled subjects to isolate and identify the separate phases of ambulation.

2. *Problems of Motivation Augmentation*

One problem, encountered upon beginning rehearsal, lay in the area of motivation level. We had previously encountered little difficulty in inhibiting haphazard ambulation attempts; but, then, with this accomplished, it was found quite difficult to induce subjects to rehearse correctly and phase by phase the various phases of ambulation. Also, when subjects eventually did complete a normal 400-stroke phase rehearsal (lasting a

(a) sinistral
monopodal
suspension

(b) dextral
thrust—
supra-
patellar

(c) dextral
thrust —
sub-
patellar

(d) torsal
inclination

(e) dextral
impact

(f) dextral
monopodal
suspension

**(g) sinistral
thrust —
supra-
patellar**

**(h) sinistral
thrust —
sub-
patellar**

**(i) torsal
inclination**

**(j) sinistral
impact**

median one hour, six minutes and six seconds), they showed great hesitation and memory blocking in identifying by name and letter the phase which they had rehearsed (it may be objected here that the subjects were preverbal; naturally this writer was aware of the difficulty involved and regarded it as one of the more challenging aspects of this study).

The problem of motivation has long been a thorny one. It has often been noted that inhibitory device technology is at a stage far advanced beyond that of motivational technology. For this reason, it was decided to apply the more sophisticated inhibitory systems to the problem of motivation augmentation. In other words, an attempt was made to instill high motivation by inhibiting low motivation. Gratifying success was encountered in this endeavor. The Tele-Algic Teaching Control Wand, in particular, although it has not yet been satisfactorily effective in remediating bad memory, has, however, shown itself a viable means of inhibiting slow or discontinuous phase rehearsal.

3. The Tele-Algic Teaching Control Wand

Slow rehearsers were, when they were observed to be lagging, subjected to 7-second bursts from the Wand; these underachievers immediately moved to a median rehearsal rate 40% higher than that which preceded use of the Wand. It was at this point decided to test, on a single subject, the upper limits of the Wand's effectiveness. The subject chosen was Wanded 33 times in an eight-hour "school" period. His rehearsal rate climbed steadily until it reached a high point nearly seven times the pre-Wanding level. At this juncture, and after emerging from a brief syncope, the subjected exhibited symptoms which led testers to postpone further work on the subject that day. However, there can be no doubt about the Wand's effectiveness; in fact, the subject showed a striking reluctance to discontinue phase rehearsal and was observed persisting in vigorous rehearsal throughout both "nutrition" and "sleep" periods. Attempts at counter inhibition with the Wand seemed only to disorient the subject and induce him to attempt unsuccessfully to increase his rehearsal rate. One day and nine hours after special Wand testing had been initiated on the subject, it was deemed necessary to reduce his rehearsal activity with Thorazine administered in standard doses at 12-hour intervals.

Such perseveration was, of course, not in evidence among the subject group as a whole, for whom Wand utilization was held to no more than eight bursts of measured pain per subject per eight-hour "school" period, each burst set at no more than 4.0 on the De Lorres Algometric Scale.

4. *The Grady System*

An equally important part in the motivation augmentation system was played by Grady's (16) Acceptance-Rejection Symbol System. Grady Symbols were assigned to subjects—in normal distribution patterns—for their achievements in rehearsal accuracy, rehearsal rate and phase-name recall. Symbol disks, of varying hues, were given by clinicians to each subject after each eight-hour "school" period. It was found that Grady motivation augmentation functioned quite similarly to the De Lorres Wand. One difference was noted, however. The Wand proved more effective for inhibiting or stimulating body movement; the Grady Symbols were more effective in controlling the more specifically cerebral activity, i.e., attempts at phase-name recall.

III. CONCLUSIONS

It is not possible at this juncture to evaluate the pilot study in question since the experiment is still in progress. However, as of this writing, one year and 301 days after the study's inception, it seems indicated to provide workers in preschool and related fields with at the least a summary of work in progress.

It is scarcely necessary to point out that any simplistic comparison of the pilot study with common, folk methods of the non-specialist would be misleading. It would be less than scientific, for example, to evaluate the pilot study approach by so naive a criterion as that of elapsed time. The fact that our subject group has not yet begun ambulation *per se* after one year and 301 days of instruction is hardly relevant here. Folk methods do, in this area, generally result in relatively rapid "success"—but the nature of this success needs to be subjected to critical analysis.

One is entitled to ask, for example, to what extent children taught to walk by "traditional" methods possess an intellectual command of their own achievement. How would they perform, say, on a Gouneigh Abstraction Test if one were devised for ambulation? To what extent are they likely to remain within acceptable deviation margins in such areas as bounce, sway, inclination and, more important, pelvic arc? And finally, what sort of ambulation instruction can they be expected to pass on to their children, having themselves been trained in so intuitive and amorphous a fashion?

Even though the pilot study is far from completed, there are grounds for cautious optimism; there is good reason to expect that the majority of our subjects will, in fact, begin ambulation and that they will do so, moreover, on the sturdy foundation provided by a thorough concept introjection. It is furthermore predicted that their standard deviations in bounce, sway, inclination and pelvic arc will be substantially less than those for the ambulatory preschool population as a whole. In fact, this writer hopes to be in a position to provide some impressive and perhaps even startling data in this area of deviation reduction.

As of this writing, the subjects are commencing prolonged rehearsal of phase (g) sinistral thrust—suprapatellar. It is appropriate at this time and in closing to express gratitude to the agencies which have made it possible to continue a project which began with less than adequate funding. In recent months, several government agencies and one private foundation, all of which have insisted on anonymity, have expressed intense interest and have proffered generous financial support. To these agencies goes our very warmest appreciation.

THE STUDENT AS NIGGER

Students are niggers. When you get that straight, our schools begin to make sense. It's more important, though, to understand why they're niggers. If we follow that question seriously enough, it will lead us past the zone of academic bullshit, where dedicated teachers pass their knowledge on to a new generation, and into the nitty-gritty of human needs and hangups. And from there we can go on to consider whether it might ever be possible for students to come up from slavery.

First let's see what's happening now. Let's look at the role students play in what we like to call education. At Cal State L.A., where I teach,* the students have separate and unequal dining facilities. If I take them into the faculty dining room, my colleagues get uncomfortable, as though there were a bad smell. If I eat in the student cafeteria, I become known as the educational equivalent of a niggerlover. In at least one building there are even rest rooms which students may not use. At Cal State, also, there is an unwritten law barring student-faculty lovemaking. Fortunately, this anti-miscegenation law, like its Southern counterpart, is not 100 percent effective.

Students at Cal State are politically disenfranchised. They are in an academic Lowndes County. Most of them can vote in national elections—their average age is about 26—but they have no voice in the decisions which affect their academic lives. The students are, it is true, allowed to have a toy government run for the

* Make that "taught."

most part by Uncle Toms and concerned principally with trivia. The faculty and administrators decide what courses will be offered; the students get to choose their own Homecoming Queen. Occasionally when student leaders get uppity and rebellious, they're either ignored, put off with trivial concessions, or maneuvered expertly out of position.

A student at Cal State is expected to know his place. He calls a faculty member "Sir" or "Doctor" or "Professor"—and he smiles and shuffles some as he stands outside the professor's office waiting for permission to enter. The faculty tell him what courses to take (in my department, English, even electives have to be approved by a faculty member); they tell him what to read, what to write, and, frequently, where to set the margins on his typewriter. They tell him what's true and what isn't. Some teachers insist that they encourage dissent but they're almost always jiving and every student knows it. Tell the man what he wants to hear or he'll fail your ass out of the course.

When a teacher says "jump," students jump. I know of one professor who refused to take up class time for exams and required students to show up for tests at 6:30 in the morning. And they did, by God! Another, at exam time, provides answer cards to be filled out— each one enclosed in a paper bag with a hole cut in the top to see through. Students stick their writing hands in the bags while taking the test. The teacher isn't a provo; I wish he were. He does it to prevent cheating. Another colleague once caught a student reading during one of his lectures and threw her book against the wall. Still another lectures his students into a stupor and then screams at them in a rage when they fall asleep.

Just last week during the first meeting of a class, one girl got up to leave after about ten minutes had gone by. The teacher rushed over, grabbed her by the arm, saying, "This class is NOT dismissed!" and led her back to her seat. On the same day another teacher began by informing his class that he does not like beards, mus-

taches, long hair on boys, or capri pants on girls, and
will not tolerate any of that in his class. The class,
incidentally, consisted mostly of high school teachers.

Even more discouraging than this master-slave approach to education is the fact that the students take
it. They haven't gone through twelve years of public
school for nothing. They've learned one thing and perhaps only one thing during those twelve years. They've
forgotten their algebra. They've grown to fear and re-
sent literature. They write like they've been loboto-
mized. But, Jesus, can they follow orders! Freshmen
come up to me with an essay and ask if I want it
folded, and whether their name should be in the upper
right hand corner. And I want to cry and kiss them and
caress their poor tortured heads.

Students don't ask that orders make sense. They give
up expecting things to make sense long before they
leave elementary school. Things are true because the
teacher says they're true. At a very early age we all
learn to accept "two truths," as did certain medieval
churchmen. Outside of class, things are true to your
tongue, your fingers, your stomach, your heart. Inside
class things are true by reason of authority. And that's
just fine because you don't care anyway. Miss Wiede-
meyer tells you a noun is a person, place or thing.
So let it be. You don't give a rat's ass; she doesn't give
a rat's ass.

The important thing is to please her. Back in kindergarten, you found out that teachers only love children
who stand in nice straight lines. And that's where it's
been at ever since. Nothing changes except to get worse.
School becomes more and more obviously a prison. Last
year I spoke to a student assembly at Manual Arts
High School and then couldn't get out of the goddamn
school. I mean there was NO WAY OUT. Locked
doors. High fences. One of the inmates was trying to
make it over a fence when he saw me coming and
froze in panic. For a moment I expected sirens, a rattle
of bullets, and him clawing the fence.

Then there's the infamous "code of dress." In some

high schools, if your skirt looks too short, you have to kneel before the principal in a brief allegory of fellatio. If the hem doesn't reach the floor, you go home to change while he, presumably, jacks off. Boys in high school can't be too sloppy and they can't even be too sharp. You'd think the school board would have been delighted to see all the black kids trooping to school in pointy shoes, suits, ties and stingy brims. Uh-uh. They're too visible.

What school amounts to, then, for white and black alike, is a 12-year course in how to be slaves. What else could explain what I see in a freshman class? They've got that slave mentality: obliging and ingratiating on the surface but hostile and resistant underneath.

As do black slaves, students vary in their awareness of what's going on. Some recognize their own put-on for what it is and even let their rebellion break through to the surface now and then. Others—including most of the "good students"—have been more deeply brainwashed. They swallow the bullshit with greedy mouths. They honest-to-God believe in grades, in busy work, in General Education requirements. They're pathetically eager to be pushed around. They're like those old grey-headed house niggers you can still find in the South who don't see what all the fuss is about because Mr. Charlie "treats us real good."

College entrance requirements tend to favor the Toms and screen out the rebels. Not entirely, of course. Some students at Cal State L.A. are expert con artists who know perfectly well what's happening. They want the degree or the 2-S and spend their years on the old plantation alternately laughing and cursing as they play the game. If their egos are strong enough, they cheat a lot. And, of course, even the Toms are angry down deep somewhere. But it comes out in passive rather than active aggression. They're unexplainably thick-witted and subject to frequent spells of laziness. They misread simple questions. They spent their nights mechanically outlining history chapters while meticulously failing to comprehend a word of what's in front of them.

The saddest cases among both black slaves and student slaves are the ones who have so thoroughly introjected their masters' values that their anger is all turned inward. At Cal State these are the kids for whom every low grade is torture, who stammer and shake when they speak to a professor, who go through an emotional crisis every time they're called upon during class. You can recognize them easily at finals time. Their faces are festooned with fresh pimples; their bowels boil audibly across the room. If there really is a Last Judgment, then the parents and teachers who created these wrecks are going to burn in hell.

So students are niggers. It's time to find out why, and to do this we have to take a long look at Mr. Charlie.

The teachers I know best are college professors. Outside the classroom and taken as a group, their most striking characteristic is timidity. They're short on balls. Just look at their working conditions. At a time when even migrant workers have begun to fight and win, most college professors are still afraid to make more than a token effort to improve their pitiful economic status. In California state colleges, the faculties are screwed regularly and vigorously by the Governor and Legislature and yet they still won't offer any solid resistance. They lie flat on their stomachs with their pants down, mumbling catch phrases like "professional dignity" and "meaningful dialogue."

Professors were no different when I was an undergraduate at UCLA during the McCarthy era; it was like a cattle stampede as they rushed to cop out. And in more recent years, I found that my being arrested in demonstrations brought from my colleagues not so much approval or condemnation as open-mouthed astonishment. "You could lose your job!"

Now, of course, there's the Vietnamese war. It gets some opposition from a few teachers. Some support it. But a vast number of professors who know perfectly well what's happening, are copping out again. And in the high schools, you can forget it. Stillness reigns.

I'm not sure why teachers are so chickenshit. It could

be that academic training itself forces a split between thought and action. It might also be that the tenured security of a teaching job attracts timid persons and, furthermore, that teaching, like police work, pulls in persons who are unsure of themselves and need weapons and the other external trappings of authority.

At any rate teachers ARE short on balls. And, as Judy Eisenstein has eloquently pointed out, the classroom offers an artificial and protected environment in which they can exercise their will to power. Your neighbors may drive a better car; gas station attendants may intimidate you; your wife may dominate you; the State Legislature may shit on you; but in the classroom, by God, students do what you say—or else. The grade is a hell of a weapon. It may not rest on your hip, potent and rigid like a cop's gun, but in the long run it's more powerful. At your personal whim—any time you choose—you can keep 35 students up for nights and have the pleasure of seeing them walk into the classroom pasty-faced and red-eyed carrying a sheaf of typewritten pages, with title page, MLA footnotes and margins set at 15 and 91.

The general timidity which causes teachers to make niggers of their students usually includes a more specific fear—fear of the students themselves. After all, students are different, just like black people. You stand exposed in front of them, knowing that their interests, their values and their language are different from yours. To make matters worse, you may suspect that you yourself are not the most engaging of persons. What then can protect you from their ridicule and scorn? Respect for authority. That's what. It's the policeman's gun again. The white bwana's pith helmet. So you flaunt that authority. You wither whisperers with a murderous glance. You crush objectors with erudition and heavy irony. And worst of all, you make your own attainments seem not accessible but awesomely remote. You conceal your massive ignorance—and parade a slender learning.

The teacher's fear is mixed with an understandable

need to be admired and to feel superior—a need which also makes him cling to his "white supremacy." Ideally, a teacher should minimize the distance between himself and his students. He should encourage them not to need him—eventually or even immediately. But this is rarely the case. Teachers make themselves high priests of arcane mysteries. They become masters of mumbo-jumbo. Even a more or less conscientious teacher may be torn between the need to give and the need to hold back, between the desire to free his students and the desire to hold them in bondage to him. I can find no other explanation that accounts for the way my own subject, literature, is generally taught. Literature, which ought to be a source of joy, solace and enlightenment, often becomes in the classroom nothing more than a source of anxiety—at best an arena for expertise, a ledger book for the ego. Literature teachers, often afraid to join a real union, nonetheless may practice the worst kind of trade-unionism in the classroom; they do to literature what Beckmesser does to song in Wagner's "Meistersinger." The avowed purpose of English departments is to teach literature; too often their real function is to kill it.

Finally, there's the darkest reason of all for the master-slave approach to education. The less trained and the less socialized a person is, the more he constitutes a sexual threat and the more he will be subjugated by institutions, such as penitentiaries and schools. Many of us are aware by now of the sexual neurosis which makes white men so fearful of integrated schools and neighborhoods, and which make the castration of Negroes a deeply entrenched Southern folkway. We should recognize a similar pattern in education. There is a kind of castration that goes on in schools. It begins before school years with parents' first encroachments on their children's free unashamed sexuality and continues right up to the day when they hand you your doctoral diploma with a bleeding, shriveled pair of testicles stapled to the parchment. It's not that sexuality has no place in the classroom. You'll find it there but only in certain perverted and vitiated forms.

How does sex show up in school? First of all, there's the sadomasochistic relationship between teachers and students. That's plenty sexual, although the price of enjoying it is to be unaware of what's happening. In walks the teacher in his Ivy League equivalent of a motorcycle jacket. In walks the teacher—a kind of intellectual rough trade—and flogs his students with grades, tests, sarcasm and snotty superiority until their very brains are bleeding. In Swinburne's England, the whipped school boy frequently grew up to be a flagellant. With us the perversion is intellectual but it's no less perverse.

Sex also shows up in the classroom as academic subject matter—sanitized and abstracted, thoroughly divorced from feeling. You get "sex education" now in both high school and college classes: everyone determined not to be embarrassed, to be very up to date, very contempo. These are the classes for which sex, as Feiffer puts it, "can be a beautiful thing if properly administered." And then, of course there's still another depressing manifestation of sex in the classroom: the "off-color" teacher who keeps his class awake with sniggering sexual allusions, obscene titters and academic innuendo. The sexuality he purveys, it must be admitted, is at least better than none at all.

What's missing, from kindergarten to graduate school, is honest recognition of what's actually happening—turned-on awareness of hairy goodies underneath the pettipants, the chinos and the flannels. It's not that sex needs to be pushed in school; sex is push enough. But we should let it be, where it is and like it is. I don't insist that ladies in junior high school lovingly caress their students' cocks (someday maybe); however, it is reasonable to ask that the ladies don't, by example and stricture, teach their students to pretend that those cocks aren't there. As things stand now, students are psychically castrated or spayed—and for the very same

reason that black men are castrated in Georgia: because
they're a threat.

So you can add sexual repression to the list of causes,
along with vanity, fear and will to power, that turn the
teacher into Mr. Charlie. You might also want to keep
in mind that he was a nigger once himself and has
never really gotten over it. And there are more causes,
some of which are better described in sociological than
in psychological terms. Work them out, it's not hard.
But in the meantime what we've got on our hands is a
whole lot of niggers. And what makes this particularly
grim is that the student has less chance than the black
man of getting out of his bag. Because the student
doesn't even know he's in it. That, more or less, is
what's happening in higher education. And the results
are staggering.

For one thing damn little education takes place in the
schools. How could it? You can't educate slaves; you
can only train them. Or, to use an even uglier and more
timely word, you can only program them.

I like to folk dance. Like other novices, I've gone to
the Intersection or to the Museum and laid out good
money in order to learn how to dance. No grades, no
prerequisites, no separate dining rooms; they just turn
you on to dancing. That's education. Now look at what
happens in college. A friend of mine, Milt, recently
finished a folk dance class. For his final, he had to learn
things like this: "The Irish are known for their wit and
imagination, qualities reflected in their dances, which
include the jig, the reel and the hornpipe." And then
the teacher graded him, A, B, C, D, or F, while he
danced in front of her. That's not education. That's not
even training. That's an abomination on the face of the
earth. It's especially ironic because Milt took that dance
class trying to get out of the academic rut. He took
crafts for the same reason. Great, right? Get your hands
in some clay? Make something? Then the teacher announced a 20-page term paper would be required—
with footnotes.

At my school we even grade people on how they

read poetry. That's like grading people on how they fuck. But we do it. In fact, God help me, I do it. I'm the Commandant of English 323. Simon Legree on the poetry plantation. "Tote that iamb! Lift that spondee!" Even to discuss a good poem in that environment is potentially dangerous because the very classroom is contaminated. As hard as I may try to turn students on to poetry, I know that the desks, the tests, the IBM cards, their own attitudes toward school, and my own residue of UCLA method are turning them off.

Another result of student slavery is equally serious. Students don't get emancipated when they graduate. As a matter of fact, we don't let them graduate until they've demonstrated their willingness—over 16 years—to remain slaves. And for important jobs, like teaching, we make them go through more years just to make sure. What I'm getting at is that we're all more or less niggers and slaves, teachers and students alike. This is a fact you might want to start with in trying to understand wider social phenomena, say, politics, in our country and in other countries.

Educational oppression is trickier to fight than racial oppression. If you're a black rebel, they can't exile you; they either have to intimidate you or kill you. But in high school or college they can just bounce you out of the fold. And they do. Rebel students and renegade faculty members get smothered or shot down with devastating accuracy. Others get tired of fighting and voluntarily leave the system. This may be a mistake though. Dropping out of college for a rebel is a little like going North for a Negro. You can't really get away from it so you might as well stay and raise hell.

How do you raise hell? That's a whole other article. But just for a start, why not stay with the analogy? What have black people done? They have, first of all, faced the fact of their slavery. They've stopped kidding themselves about an eventual reward in that Great Watermelon Patch in the sky. They've organized; they've decided to get freedom now, and they've started taking it.

Students, like black people, have immense unused power. They could, theoretically, insist on participating in their own education. They could make academic freedom bilateral. They could teach their teachers to thrive on love and admiration, rather than fear and respect, and to lay down their weapons. Students could discover community. And they could learn to dance by dancing on the IBM cards. They could make coloring books out of the catalogs and they could put the grading system in a museum. They could raze one set of walls and let life come blowing into the classroom. They could raze another set of walls and let education flow out and flood the streets. They could turn the classroom into where it's at—a "field of action" as Peter Marin describes it. And believe it or not, they could study eagerly and learn prodigiously for the best of all possible reasons—their own reasons.

They could. Theoretically. They have the power. But only in a very few places, like Berkeley, have they even begun to think about using it. For students, as for black people, the hardest battle isn't with Mr. Charlie. It's with what Mr. Charlie has done to your mind.

DOING TIME IN NEW COUNTY

(To the memory of Michael Robinson)

At night after lights out we'd talk. It was always the best time for talking. Other scenes would take shape and float in the dark: the streets, women, good food, other jails. And you learned a lot in those aimless conversations: basic stuff, like how many lids in a ki and how to strip a car—and more advanced techniques, like how to use the Escobedo decision, how to screw up a Nalline test, where to stash.

The cell was less strangulating at night, almost roomy enough for the four of us. Laird would usually have fallen asleep. And Ramon was usually talking. He was a skinny, relaxed chicano with Moonbeam McSwine on his back and an Indian princess on his chest. Stretched out in the dark under his cigarette, his eyes half shut, Ramon talked softly about the waterfront where he worked, about his first piece of ass, about narcos, parole officers, whorehouses in TJ, his jealous wife, his time at Chino.

When Ramon went to Chino, they put him in the placement center and ran him through the usual series of tests and interviews. He was disgusted by the psychiatrists.

"You wouldn't believe the questions, man. Did I screw my sister, fuck cousins, have nightmares? What kind of questions is that? Is that why a man goes to college and all that and studies to be a doctor and all that to talk that shit? I told him not to talk to me like that! Man, he asked did I screw my sister—like I was some kind of dummy. So I just dummied up. Fuck him."

Joe, another chicano, just out of his teens, was in the bunk below me. He generally stayed up while we talked, but he said very little. Especially when Ramon and I talked pussy—which we usually did—Joe was quiet, taking it all in.

Sometimes, lying there in the dark, we'd hear from other cells. Every night, late, a brother somewhere in Charlie Row below would lay down "I'll Take Romance," "Stella By Starlight," "Green Dolphin Street" and more until his country-and-western cellmates made him stop it. (More than once at New County I caught the faint echo of old prison movies. There's a lot of pop art in jail. They call the chaplain a "sky pilot.")

Now and then during the night Nathan the Claw, from next door, would have something to say. Nathan was a mean, wiry Russian Jew. He was around fifty-five or sixty, with a dragging limp and a congenitally deformed hand, which was three-digited and deeply cleft. He had done a total of thirty years in the joint for robbing mail trucks, and was now facing trial for allegedly having stabbed a waiter eight times with a steak knife (strangely enough, without having done him any permanent damage). One particular night, shortly after lights out, Nathan started chuckling. He called out to our cell.

"Hey, number four."

"What?"

"Listen to this. I'm the Crippled Creeper. Sometime I'm going to reach up in the middle of the night and choke the life out of somebody."

His cellmates did a lot of their sleeping in the daytime. And I never called him Nathan the Claw to his face.

Nathan was the bitterest man I've ever met. "You kill a couple of lousy motherfuckers," he used to say, "and they call you a fuckin' homicidal maniac."

Sooner or later we'd all be asleep—even Nathan and his cellmates. And then, a few hours later—at 5:30—

all hell would break loose. There would be barred gates banging open and shut down an infinite perspective of sound. Toilets flushing all around. Waterpipes ringing. An epidemic of coughing, spitting, groaning. Bright lights on like waking up in surgery or like enemy flares for a night attack. And the loudspeaker in an unending barrage: "2500, are you clear? 2600, CHOW TIME! Baker Row, form a line. Watch the GATES, Charlie Row!"

I'd wait for the last possible minute, then scoop up my shirt and shoes and stumble out onto the "freeway," as the electrically controlled cell gate crashed shut behind me. There'd be plenty of time to sit on the guard rail and finish dressing, eyes closed against the glare— maybe a ten-minute wait. Then we'd trudge, glassy-eyed and half asleep, out of the row, down the stairs and through the halls. Then into the chowroom, past the slop buckets, and through the mess line to sit at long steel tables, where we had maybe eight minutes for morning chow. It was hard to tell how long they let us stay because the chowroom clocks didn't work. They'd been stopped, I heard, several months back because the inmates had gotten mean about a 6-minute dinner period.

Not that the chow was anything to linger and pick your teeth over. It was foul—not bad from negligence but, as they say in court, willfully and with intent. We ate from metal plates with tablespoons. Nothing was served that couldn't be handled with a spoon. (The reasoning behind this seemed to be that if you wanted to cut someone, you would have to use the razor blades on sale at the commissary window.) So the diet was slop, and mostly starch. Once a week, though, we got "Gainesburgers," tough, tasteless disks like big, thick scabs. Coffee and tea were almost indistinguishable— equally bad, always bitter and sugarless. The bread was dry, white and evil; sometimes it came with a jelly called Red Death, which was left untouched by all but the newly arrived and the desperately constipated.

Our trips to and from chow remained bewildering to

me for some time. It's almost impossible to keep any sense of direction when you're in New County, which is a huge, automated, maximum security universe of featureless cell blocks and nightmare corridors. Imagine "Last Year at Marienbad" written by Kafka. The first time they took me to my cell at New County I was utterly disoriented. Amplified voices boomed out of the wall directing me as I walked through bare corridors. Then through a door or around a corner into more corridors. And electrically operated steel doors were slamming closed behind me all the time. I passed through a set of corridor gates. Slam. They took me to my module. Crash. They took me to my row. Clang. They put me in the cell. Thud. Once you're in it's hopeless—like being locked in a set of nested Chinese boxes.

Cell blocks in New County are called "modules" (it's startling how many vogue words turn up in jail—by now cops are probably referring to interrogation as "dialogue"). A module is four rows of cells, set back to back in two layers, like the Stack Packs in a pound box of Saltines. The upper layer includes a shower area; the lower one has a desk with bull, loudspeaker and pushbutton control board, and a commissary window. During my last stay in New County, I was in Denver, an upper row in Module 2600. It consisted of a dozen four-man cells with remote-controlled gates that opened onto the freeway, a four-foot-wide cement walkway. The barred cell gates would slide open and shut noisily and irresistibly to the accompaniment of ritual warning calls by the row's trusties ("They're coming HOME, Denver Row!"). Despite these calls, someone would periodically get caught by a gate and sent to the infirmary.

If you're not a trusty you're locked up in the cell day and night, except for chow time, shower time and store time. And, if you have visitors, you can go downstairs once a day on weekdays to face them through a thick glass window and talk to them over a remote-controlled phone which goes dead when your time is up. But almost all of the time you're in your cell, which is roughly six by ten or maybe eleven feet and which contains two double-decker bunks, a washbasin and a toilet with no seat. In the daytime and before lights out you can play cards, smoke, talk or read. James Bond was very big when I was in New County last summer; the entire Fleming canon was kept in motion up and down the row by barter, theft and kindness.

There was also a small visiting library which came once a week and which did a hell of a business, especially in poetry. My copies of Keats and Housman had been checked out every week for the previous year. I've never seen such an audience for poetry. Every day, until my memory ran dry, I would recite poems to my cell mates, to the trusties or to the next door neighbors. If anyone particularly liked a poem ("I sing of Olaf" was popular) I'd write out a copy. They dug the poetry and I was where they scored for it. Denver Row was a very classy row with nothing but Federal beefs, and almost everyone on the row was a connection of some sort. Ford taught bullfighting; Moffit stashed candy bars for weekends when there was no store; Norris taught writs and courtroom procedure; Arturo drew dirty pictures; Ramon told stories; Nathan hipped you to the joint, if that's where you were headed.

Once you're settled in a cell at New County, you're in continual contact with other inmates but you see very little of the bulls. Communication is over loud-speakers and is pretty well automated except for when they beat somebody. The fact that you're mostly out of personal touch with the jailers is one of New County's chief assets, along with the absence of rats, thumb-screws and the rack. If you want to get a good look at the bulls, the time to do it is during the booking process which you go through when you first arrive. Let me tell you about that, and about Marquez, the Deputy.

First, picture the scene. New arrivals—who are called "fish," perhaps because of their collective rank smell —spend most of their booking time waiting in one after another of a series of barred enclosures called holding tanks. So you're in a tank with fifty or so fish, still motley and exotic in their street threads. A number of fish have obviously been in these threads for days, probably on a binge. Some poor bastard has usually crapped in his pants—because of drinking, or maybe because of fear. In any case, there are always a few drunks down, hugging the tank's concrete floor, fighting DT's. Other fish are obvious losers of fights, and they hunch over on benches, hurting. The old timers loll expertly, waiting. The sweet stink that stems up from all of these bodies may be nasty, but still it's unregenerate and soulful and all you have going for you. After showering, when the smell goes, they've got you; you ain't even shit.

In New County the first few booking tanks are Marquez' kingdom—or at least they were last June. Marquez the Deputy is always on stage, badmouthing his wretched captive audience. He's got cropped blonde hair and a young burly body. He wears surgical rubber gloves and hitches them up continually like the Interrogator in a World War II movie ("So, American swine —you will not talk?").

Marquez typically chooses a scapegoat or two out of every batch. The last time in I thought at first he had chosen me. When I sat down on a bench, he ambled over, tightening his gloves.

"Move over, asshole! I want seven on that bench."

So I jammed up against the drunk next to me, who was easing off his shoes with quivering hands and who then began to pick the most black deposits from between his toes. "Maybe," I thought, "I'm the one this time." Because shortly before, when another bull had found out where I work and that I was busted for sitting in at the Federal Building, he had looked up smiling.

"I guess you've lost your job at the college, Farber. You're washed up."

"No, I've still got a job."

"Not when they find out. You're fired, buddy."

"They know, they know. This was my seventh arrest."

"Bullshit. They're going to fire your ass, mother-fucker!"

It was a matter of faith with him. And it began to seem that I was the one to get hassled this time. But Marquez had picked another target: Gwinn, a toothless stubbly old wino with big flashing eyes like Ethel Barrymore's. Gwinn, who seemed uncertain where he was, was losing a debate with Marquez.

"Gwinn, you old prick. Get out your property envelope."

"Shit, I ain't got no envelope."

"Watch your mouth, cocksucker!"

"Well, shit, I lost the motherfucker."

Marquez looked at us with theatrical exasperation. He pulled the envelope out of Gwinn's pocket and took him into the next room. We hear Marquez shout, "Go ahead, motherfucker, open your mouth," then heard a couple of loud slaps. The drunk next to me, still mining his toes, mumbled, "Goddamn Nazi." Someone walked over to look through the small glass window in the door. But, as he got there, a bull in the next room put a coat over the window; we heard another series of slaps.

Gwinn was already naked under a shower when we were herded into the next room. He was bathed in water—not fire—but still I remember him as the very image of Dante's Farinata, snotty and unrepentant in the flaming sepulchre (I'm sorry—but if you're going to send literature teachers to jail, that's the sort of shit you'll have to put up with).

Marquez was still screaming at him: "Stay where you are, motherfucker, or I'll knock your goddamn head off."

After the shower, new inmates get sprayed with pesticide and dressed in prison blues. Then they're fingerprinted, X-rayed, bled and given a short-arm check. But just before showering, they leave their street clothes to be searched and stand naked in a long line. A bull walks past, peeping in mouths, under arms, up assholes.

"Bend over and spread 'em." This time the rectum

inspector stopped as he passed one tall blood and said angrily, "God damn—that's shit!"

Brother, still bent over, asked, "What did y'all expect? Ice Cream?"

The bull slapped him on the ass and went on down the line.

That's booking. Just more of that crap for a very long time—at best four or five hours, but more likely twelve to fifteen hours or longer. It's the closest thing to torture New County has to offer—unless you're unlucky enough to get beat or sent to the hole during your stay. Once an inmate gets past booking, he may even run into an occasional bull who acts human. Like Vellardo, the bull who ran our module on the swing shift. He wasn't a patsy. But he wasn't uptight. He laughed sometimes; he made up funny, not too hostile pseudonyms for the trusties. That's all. But next to Marquez and the others, he looked pretty good.

Fairness demands that I give Vellardo a nod. But the most striking contrasts weren't to be found among the bulls but rather between the bulls and the inmates. That's why trips to jail over three or four years mess up your mind and desocialize you. That's why you can think of yourself as a criminal without feeling shame. Our society, on the whole, never appears particularly groovy or human or honest; in jail, personified by the bulls, it looks like sick shit. The inmates are something else. They may fall into categories at first—splib, paddy, beaner, junky—but you get past the categories pretty easily and reach persons, unique and desperately valuable like yourself. With the jailers, you almost never get past their Orwellian role. They're so goddamn easy to hate. So the bulls become the villains and the inmates the good guys. What jail amounts to, then, is a high-powered Skinnerian conditioner. You go in somebody who got caught or screwed or maybe just pulled in off the streets, and you come out a righteous Capital C no-shit Criminal. Jail drops you out but usually without turning you on and tuning you in—and that's too bad.

I say "usually." While we're talking about criminals, let's look at Norris, one of the trusties in Denver Row. In Folsom, doing a 1 to 10 for allegedly dealing in grass, he had become a Buddhist. It had started with some casual reading in the library. Soon he began getting books on Eastern religion sent in—he accumulated several hundred, in time. Norris shaved his head, improvised a sort of meditation mat, spent hours a day in the lotus position, stopped smoking and masturbating, and decided that jail was not so different from anywhere else—the walls were more obvious, that was all. After a time he began to correspond with leading Buddhists all over the world and to subscribe to the various Buddhist journals.

The whole scene almost blew up when the authorities got a letter for Norris from the daughter of the Maharaja of Sikkim. "Why don't you hang up all this shit, Norris, and become a Christian?" the captain asked him. And the captain threatened to require the Sikkimese princess to fill out an arrest-record correspondence form. Finally, the assistant warden interceded and allowed the correspondence to go on. Norris, incidentally, wangled the first and probably last subscription to *Evergreen Review* in Folsom history.

Another trusty—and my closest friend on Denver Row—was Ford who, before he was busted, had been way up on the FBI's hit parade in connection with a series of alleged bank robberies. According to Ford, he had been traveling from Miami to Los Angeles to turn himself in and fight the case when a hayseed cop in Oklahoma hit it lucky and took him in. Whether Ford was a bank robber and, if so, how many of the alleged robberies were his I can't say; we never discussed the circumstances behind his case.

Ford was a brilliant hipster, an ex-sailor and ex-matador, thin, nervous, with a black Van Dyke beard and a nourishing, inexhaustible disgust for the FBI and its chief. Ford refused to stop grooving—even in jail, wearing miserable, inelegant prison blues and facing 22 felony counts. He transformed them all.

Because he was a trusty, Ford could roam up and down the freeway. We spent hours at a time talking through the bars of my cell. He liked to read us the paper out loud, interpolating effortlessly as he read:

". . . these and related crimes climbed sharply during the first quarter of 1965, according to Bureau Chief G. Edward Homosexual Motherfucking Cigar-Smoking Takes-it-in-the-ass Hooper. Other statistics reveal . . ."

Ford had a family in Mexico. His wife wrote him warm, loyal and optimistic letters, which delighted him and depressed the hell out of me because I kept thinking how long it might be before he would be home again. Occasionally something depressed Ford, but not often. His fantastic style devoured obstacles. It was probably his sense of style that had turned him on to bullfighting. Also, I imagine, his passion for trouble.

One day Ramon's and my questions generated a sort of lecture-demonstration on the history of the bullfight that lasted most of the afternoon. Here, Ford explained, was what Belmonte had done. Here was what Manolete had introduced. Bulls hurtled up and down the freeway that afternoon as he went on to deal with Arruza, then Dominguin, then El Cordobes. Afterward, when Ford left to go back to his cell, Ramon and I went on talking. And as I talked, with my face against the bars, I was just barely able to see Ford performing a splendid series of passes right down the freeway to the front gate. He stopped, his arms at his sides, his non-existent cape dragging on the cement, and stared at the barred gate briefly. Then, contemptuously, he turned his back on it and walked confidently away.

I remember Ford very well. And Norris. And Ramon. And the others. Does it sound like I'm making heroes out of them? I guess I am.

I remember them all. Though by now perhaps I have to dig a little for the memories. What comes to my mind most easily still—unsought and often—is not the image of persons or even of the cell I lived in. What comes to my mind is sound. Sounds in jail are freer, more mysterious, more communal than other impressions.

Vellardo on the loudspeaker: "Baker Row: Green Hornet get down here!" Soul brother on Charlie Row singing "Green Dolphin Street" at two in the morning. Ford shouting to Vellardo when it was time to close the gates: "Denver Row is clear, sir" and occasionally "Denver Row is queer, sir," and, as they started to close, "They're coming HOME, Denver Row." Ramon murmuring in the dark like harbor water. The sounds of toilets flushing and men hacking and coughing, and iron gates opening and closing far off in the endless identical automated maximum-security cells, rows and modules of New County Jail.

LOVE DUEL AT CRYSTAL SPRINGS

(Note: Let my anti-hippie readers take no comfort from this satire. That whole scene was beautiful, and, *at worst,* funny, while so many other scenes are ludicrous at best.)

Much of L.A.'s vast underground community is still not hip to an unusual and significant tribal gathering that took place in the Crystal Springs area of Griffith Park last Saturday. Two of our very groovy local tribes met there at dawn in a sort of unpublicized love-in to celebrate and arrange a tribal merger.

Like everyone who attended I was so flipped out behind all of it that I have since had trouble describing what happened. But I want to try just the same because anything as groovy, as mythic, as loving and as Traditional as this just has to be shared.

First, can you dig the scene? Before dawn—when the two groups were to meet—Lord Fairfax's tribe was encamped on the flat grassy area near the road and Marco's people were spread out on the slopes just beyond. Until it began to get light, all you could see were a couple of small fires and, around them, moving here and there in the dark, the glowing tips of joints and incense sticks. There were also a number of flickering perfumed tapers, which both Marco and Lord Fairfax used to sanctify various pre-dawn tribal ceremonies. Marco performed several marriages as well as a briss and a divorce. Lord Fairfax did two marriages, granted one temporary restraining order and accepted a plea of nolo contendere on a matter carried over from the previous Sunday's love-in.

All of this took place before the sun came up. When the light finally did appear, both tribes greeted it with the Hare Krishna mantra, of which Allen Ginsberg says, "It brings a state of ecstasy!" After the mantra, Elliot Mintz read a telegram in which Allen expressed his regret at not being able to be present but sent his best vibrations. Elliot also introduced the persons who made the tribal gathering possible, and up front made a plea for everyone to help pick up trash before going home in the evening.

By the time this holy morning raga ended it was light enough to trip out on the beautiful scene. Marco's tribe had come down from the slopes and was standing in a body facing Lord Fairfax's people on the flat grassy area. They looked a lot like two small armies ready for battle—and indeed they were, but these were armies of the future, baby, carrying no weapons but love and beauty (In fact when the uptight materialistic white world of fear-ridden brown-shoes, power-trip politicians and hate-filled police blows itself up in an orgasmic Armageddon and at last pays for its crimes against the Traditional American Indian, then it will be just such love armies of gentle seed-carrying hippies with their black and red flower brothers who will wander triumphantly across the earth like freaked-out nonviolent Mongol hordes).

Now in order for you to dig what was going down, I have to explain the merger ritual. You see, each tribe before the merger had its own spiritual leader; Marco was one and Lord Fairfax was the other. But after the merger they would be one tribe, and it was generally agreed that any single tribe with two spiritual leaders would be sent on a bummer. "Too many yogin," as Marco put it, "spoil the pirogen." So part of the merger ritual—in fact the main part—was sort of an elimination thingy to cut down on spiritual leaders, leaving just one, with the other becoming you know like a sidekick. Now the square uptight way of solving this kind of problem would be some kind of armed combat or at best some viciously competitive civil service exam. But the two tribes chose to let it happen lovingly and to let their gurus compete—if you want to use the word "compete" at all—in love. You dig? Marco and Lord Fairfax, two of the most beautiful cats in Southern California, in an eyeball-to-eyeball love duel.

So there, in the cool incense-fragrant dawn, were these two tribes, facing each other across the still damp grassy field, getting ready, turning on in an aura of gentle pagan sound: flute, drum and tambourine. There was about a 15-yard stretch of ground between the tribes, who were beaming love at each other through the patterned psychedelic air. It was an earth thing, an ancient mythic thing. Mr. Jones, take a good look! Here were the New Americans! Sterling silver roach holders dangled from intricately beaded Traditional American Indian-style belts. Custom-made knee length rawhide boots with fringed tops alternated with massive and ornate all-leather sandals. Everyone had his button collection on. Everyone wore bright short dresses with colorful tights or multi-colored striped shirts and pants or bright long robes. Everyone carried toys to look at or look through or play with. Every single person wore handcrafted jewelry and bead necklaces supporting glittering gems or emblems in metal or wood. It was Groovy New America giving the lie to Materialistic Conformist Old America.

Then the two rock bands began to do their thing. Marco's band, The Warren Commission, took turns with Lord Fairfax's group, The Cherokee Omelet. In preparation for and as a symbol of the coming merger, they had figured out a way to wire up both sets of amplifiers so that their maximum volume was doubled. Are you ready for that? Doubled? It was pure McLuhan, baby. When The Warren Commission did their thing, they transformed Griffith Park, Silverlake, Echo Park, Glendale, Eagle Rock and Burbank into a tribal village right on the spot. And when The Cherokee

Omelet took over, it was a mind-blower you wouldn't believe. They just had to be laying down the genetic code, man. The two-billion-year-old genetic code itself. It couldn't have been anything else. I haven't checked this out but I've heard that when The Cherokee Omelet played their first number, three soldiers stationed at a Nike missile base in the Hollywood Hills took off their uniforms, burned them and walked off the job naked with flowers in their hair. If anyone has more information on this, I'd appreciate hearing from him.

So the rock groups played and everybody freaked out dancing. Imagine: It's like seven in the morning—still pretty cold and gray. The musicians are laying down more sound in five minutes than the average career artilleryman hears in a lifetime. And around them on the grass are 100 cases of apparent epilepsy. Can you dig it? We just let it happen, man.

Finally, at a certain point, the music stopped dead. Everything stopped. There wasn't a sound, except for a little breeze in the leaves, like in "Blow-Up." Then Lord Fairfax stepped out in front of his tribe and walked forward, his bells jangling like spurs. It was time for the two to do their thing. But first let me hip you to what they looked like.

Marco? I can't describe it. He was too beautiful, man. Can you dig a violet leather mini-sari with Traditional American Indian fringework? He was wearing one, man. Chartreuse tights on his legs. And shoes? Are you ready? Pilgrim Father Buckle Shoes! It was beautiful. And ankhs? Godseyes? Yin-Yangs? Mandalas? Beads? Talismans? Amulets? Charms? The cat could HARDLY MOVE, man! I mean this was a very beautiful cat. And I haven't even mentioned his buttons. "Let's Suck Toes"—"Undergo Lysurgery"—"Down to Lunch"—you name it and he was wearing it. Plus a complete set of Ron Boise Kama Sutra Sculpture buttons, each position set against a background of I Ching hexagrams, astrological signs and Tarot symbols.

Now if Marco was beautiful, Lord Fairfax was just AS beautiful. It wasn't his clothes because he didn't have any on—except for a Traditional Borneo Indian penis sheath, which was also long enough to keep a stash in (You get them at The Yoni in Bell Gardens). What he had on was groovy body paint. Like on his chest, in pale rose on an umber ground, it said "LOVE" —but in lettering so psychedelic—dig this—in lettering so psychedelic that the cat who did it *can't even read what he wrote*. And he won't be able to either until the next time he gets that high. At exactly 983 mikes you can read what the lettering says. One mike less and it's totally meaningless. Across Lord Fairfax's back was "BORN TO LOSE" in traditional Red, White and Blue with three eagles vert and, on a bend sable, five martlets or. And his buns, man. On his left was a really delicate watercolor of Bodhidharma regarding a plum blossom. And on his right was a silk-screened reproduction of a photo of Jerry ("Captain Trips") Garcia turning on with the Hopi. Between them, up his ass, was a lit stick of incense ("Nirvana"—which you can score at the Kazoo).

So there they are, baby—mano a mano. In front of one tribe is Lord Fairfax with his long wavy brown hair and beard, standing tall and dreamy like some kind of saint on a church wall in Borneo. And in front of the other tribe is Marco, a lot shorter, smiling, with flowers in his mouth and flowers twined in his blond beard, and with the eternal Atman gazing out through his trippy blue eyes.

The two cats stared at each other lovingly; they were beginning to do their thing. Neither one wavered or blinked or even got watery eyed. In fact, it was just the opposite. As time passed . . . ten minutes . . . fifteen minutes . . . a half hour . . . their thing got more intense and more loving. The ordinary cat couldn't have taken that kind of heavy trip. They would have loved him to death.

In fact, if you didn't have your head together, you couldn't even bear being in the vicinity. Like the narks.

They couldn't take it. After 30 minutes of those good vibrations, the plainclothes cops completely blew their cool. No matter how freaky their threads were, or how much acid they had dropped, or how tight they were with the tribes, the narks just had to split. They were clutching their throats, man! The cats were SCREAMING! Aargh! Aargh! And they ran back to the squad cars parked on the road. It was like when Dracula sees the cross on the chick's neck, man. They just weren't ready for that kind of love.

I'm sure you can dig that there were some surprises that morning. Like four of Lord Fairfax's dancers ran off to the squad cars, gnawing on their badges. And Marco's wife? A nark! Can you believe it? Marco's WIFE, man! That morning at Crystal Springs was the moment of truth. If you were the heat, or even if you were just a weekend hippy, it was tough titty on you.

But dig. None of this even reached Marco and Lord Fairfax. I may have noticed the cops splitting. The tribes may have noticed them; in fact there were a great many rocks and bottles thrown (thrown, I should add, not in anger but in love). But Marco and Fairfax just kept up that love stare. Lord Fairfax's incense even burned down but he didn't seem to notice it. They went on for another half hour. Then Lord Fairfax spoke. He said:

"You're a beautiful cat."

I guess you could say that it was sort of Marco's move. But he didn't say anything. He stared up at Lord Fairfax for a long time, squinting his stoned blue eyes in the sun. Maybe another half hour went by. Then Marco asked:

"What did you say man?"

"I said you're beautiful."

"Oh." Marco didn't say anything else for another long time. Finally he took Lord Fairfax's hand and squeezed it and said slowly, "I can't tell you, man. It's too beautiful. You may not know it but you've just changed my life."

Now you would have thought that nobody could be

laying down more love than Lord Fairfax. But Marco's gratitude. Marco's beautiful gratitude! It was too much. You had to cry, man. And meanwhile the play was kind of tossed back to Lord Fairfax.

But Fairfax was right in there playing heads-up ball. He reached out with his other hand, gently touching Marco's face, and he said, "Marco, it's the you in me that's changed the you in you."

What a trip! Lord Fairfax was all love and admiration and yet the kind of deep talk he was laying down left you wondering if maybe Marco was too lightweight intellectually to be a spiritual leader. And yet you felt that Lord Fairfax in his humility thought himself the lesser cat. It was too much.

Now metaphysics was never Marco's bag so no one was surprised when he didn't try to top Lord Fairfax in the "you-in-me" thing. But still, what Marco did say— "Teach me, man"—seemed unnecessarily weak. Like he was dwelling on what he should have been staying away from. And Marco's people started to look a little nervous. "Teach me" seemed like asking for trouble.

Even Lord Fairfax looked puzzled. But he smiled and said, "There is nothing to teach and nothing to learn."

Some people I've talked to say they felt at that point that Lord Fairfax was walking into a trap. But I don't think so. It wasn't that kind of thing. It was too beautiful.

Anyway, Marco said softly, "Nothing to teach and nothing to learn. What is there then?"

Lord Fairfax didn't answer right away. He walked back to where his tribe was and came back with a basket of tangerines. He handed them to Marco. "Love," he said.

Now there was something going down that Lord Fairfax couldn't have known because nobody knew except some of the kids in Marco's tribe. You see, Marco couldn't eat tangerines when he was stoned. They put him on a big nausea trip. But here he was all the same with a love gift of tangerines. The cat was in trouble. He looked at them for a minute. Then he started passing them out to his tribe. But after everyone had taken theirs, there were still some left over. So he bit into one. The kids who were hip to his tangerine problem came running up to stop him but he waved them away. "One swallow," he said with his mouth full, "doesn't make a bummer."

Marco might have looked a little green. But if he was nauseated, he maintained. He smiled up at Lord Fairfax and said, "You're right, man. Love IS what's happening. I love you. I give you my tribe."

Fantastic! Marco was really looking good in there! It was Lord Fairfax's move and, if you thought about it, you knew he only had one. It was like chess, man. There was only one answer he could make. He said, "Marco, I'm glad you gave me your tribe because now I can make you a gift of both tribes. You are a beautiful, loving cat. You are our spiritual leader."

Almost at once everyone there began to realize that Marco had blown it. Because if Marco's giving one tribe made him a beautiful, loving cat, then Lord Fairfax had come through as a twice-as-beautiful, twice-as-loving cat by giving two tribes. And what's more, Fairfax had made the ultimate move. Like you couldn't top it. Marco had set up his own checkmate. The cat was in real trouble now.

There was a silent wait. Everyone was trying to figure out what Marco could do and was feeling maybe a little sorry for him. But Marco looked very cool. And then he said, suddenly:

"Why thank you, I accept. Thank you very much. Very kind of you." And he nodded quickly to The Warren Commission, which immediately went into a very freaky thing that had everybody dancing in seconds.

Everybody, that is, except Lord Fairfax, who was standing there looking at Marco. Marco kissed him and said, "My first action as spiritual leader of the combined tribes is to appoint you Tribe Metaphysician and Love Fountain."

But Lord Fairfax was on a weird trip. In fact, it was

15 or 20 minutes before he walked over to Marco, who was dancing, and asked:

"What did you say?"

Still dancing, Marco repeated, "I accept and I appoint you Metaphysician and Love Fountain."

"Oh. Groovy." Lord Fairfax nodded his head to the music. "Groovy," he said again. "Groovy." He walked away, still nodding his head, to get a tangerine. "That's groovy." He peeled it. "Yeah, that's pretty damn groovy all right." Meanwhile, everyone was dancing.

This past week there's been some grumbling among the people who had been in Lord Fairfax's tribe. A couple of them have said that maybe Marco copped out on the love thing. There's even been some talk about running a full-page put-down of Marco in the *Free Press*. But Marco meanwhile has consolidated his position very quickly. His new tribe has already received official recognition from such tribes as the L.A. Oracle and Hugh Romney's Hog Farm people. Marco is also working out a consular treaty with Vito's Fraternity of Man, and he has been laying a lot of canned goods on Plastic Man and the other diggers.

As for what people are now referring to as the "love duel," Marco doesn't say too much. But yesterday, when I was rapping with him about it, he opened up a little. He said that it was possible that Lord Fairfax had been a little straighter than him that day but that there was such a thing as being too straight.

"Too much dharma," Marco said, "spoils the karma." And he told me his private opinion of Lord Fairfax, which was that Fairfax was indeed a beautiful, loving cat but maybe a little too loving and too beautiful to be a good administrator.

AUGUST, 1965

"What the hell do the police want?" someone asked.

About 25 squad cars had entirely blocked off Avalon at the corner of Imperial Highway. Policemen and motorcycles lined the street. A growing crowd jammed the sidewalk.

"A riot."

"They gonna get one."

The police had to wait quite a while for their riot. At 11, when we arrived from the N-VAC office, they had already been there maybe an hour. And when we reached the intersection, there was still nothing happening, except that the crowd was growing larger every minute. People had heard about the situation—it was already on television and radio—and were coming to watch. They stood on bus benches or on trucks in the Shell station to get a better view. It was like a parade but with angry spectators. Six of us from N-VAC circulated in the crowd for nearly an hour asking questions. Earlier in the evening, we learned, there had been some rock throwing along Avalon just south of Imperial. Most of the persons we talked to said that it had all started when the police had kicked and slugged a woman. A few insisted that the woman had been pregnant.

Finally—it must have been close to midnight—someone threw a rock. It hit a squad car. A minute or two later a bottle crashed in the street and the newsmen began to leave. From this point on it becomes difficult to remember the sequence of events. But individual scenes are very vivid in my mind. A policeman started to drive his squad car away and someone threw a cigarette butt in it. He stopped, opened the door, located the cigarette and tossed it out. He looked around at the hostile crowd and said, "Thanks a lot!" How can I explain how he said it? He wanted to *get* our ass so bad—but he was afraid. And since he was afraid, he made like it was just a little joke. For me, that was when the whole thing started.

I remember that the tempo of rock and bottle throwing gradually increased. There was also a lot of shouting. I saw a girl about 15 screaming, almost in tears, "*Fuck you,* cop! *Fuck you!*" Finally, 15 or 20 policemen rushed the crowd with their clubs swinging. They didn't get the rock throwers, who were in back; they grabbed two or three kids out of the crowd and arrested them. During another of these flying raids by the police, I saw someone go down and saw four or five policemen beating him, swinging their clubs high in the air.

At one point, a dozen or so policemen stood in a line facing 40 or 50 of us in the gas station. A couple of them were spinning and twirling their clubs in what they must have regarded as a menacing manner. Someone in the crowd called out, "Hey, you're looking GOOD, motherfucker!" Someone else just missed them with a rock. The police made another rush into the crowd. We scattered; they were arresting, and frequently beating, anyone they could catch. Caroline (also from N-VAC) and I made it over a fence into a back yard next to the Shell station. A man came out of his back door, pointed a pistol at us and said, "I told all of you to get out of my yard. Now get!" I tried to explain about the police but he wasn't listening; he kept waving his damn pistol at me. So we jumped the fence back into the gas station and hid under a truck while the cops rushed around with their clubs in the air.

A little later we emerged and looked around. Robert Hall showed up, furious. He had been taking notes for N-VAC. A cop had ripped the notes out of his hand and torn them up.

At some point after the rock throwing started, the police left. The motorcycle cops took off in a noisy razzle-dazzle—making loops in tight formation near the intersection. It was like a shooting gallery as people in the crowd tried to score with rocks. When the police left, the rock and bottle throwers began checking out passing cars, looking for whitey. Any brother who drove by slowly, holding out a Watts or Compton or Slauson hand signal, was usually safe. The rest were targets; it was hard to make out the color of a driver speeding by at night.

Across the street one group caught a UPI newsman, Nick Beck, in a phone booth and began beating him. Robert Hall pushed his way through, got Beck out of the booth and into his car.

A KTTV mobile unit had been abandoned on the corner. Some kids rolled it onto its side and then, with great effort, on its top. It immediately burst into flames, which lit the entire intersection. A middle-aged lady next to me was talking to a man who had been near the car.

"Look what they done. Somebody in there?"

"No, it's all right. Ain't nobody inside."

"Ain't that something? That truck is burning *up!*"

She was smiling. A lot of people were smiling. The rebellion was well under way.

When we left, around 2:30 a.m., a pattern of guerrilla warfare had been set. There were bands of neighborhood people—teenagers and young men—throwing bottles and rocks at passing cars and beating up whites who stopped and got out of their cars (for hours I had been expecting the police to block off that section of Imperial Highway but they never did). When police came our way, whatever groups were on the street would disappear into houses and yards or would take up a position further down.

Robert and I got a lift back to N-VAC with a photographer from *Muhammad Speaks*. On our way to the car we stopped by a group of rock throwers. One of them, with conked hair, his T-shirt cut off at the sleeves, said, "We been getting hit a long time. Now we hitting back."

He wanted to know what paper the photographer was from. When he found out, he said, "Well listen, man, tell it like it is."

"That's the only thing we print in *Muhammad Speaks,* brother—how it *is.* What are you going to do now?"

"We going to get every white motherfucker comes down this street." He kept glancing up the dark, empty boulevard, looking for cars, looking for the police.

"Listen, brother, the Honorable Elijah Muhammad's been telling you about the devils for years. You brothers got to come on down to the mosque and get with it."

"Ain't no need to go down there. I got my business right here. You understand? I'm ready to die! You know what I mean? But don't get me wrong. You got a point, brother, you got a point."

By the next night, Thursday, the people of Watts were in possession of a good part of their own community. A carload from N-VAC drove over in the early evening. This time there weren't any white skins in the car. The night before, five white kids had come down. Four of them barely made it out. Dave, convicted, ironically, earlier that day for a civil rights demonstration, had been caught by a group of teenagers. He curled up in the nonviolent position, was kicked a few times and left alone. The fifth Caucasian, Caroline Sweezy, was there almost as long as Robert and I, and had remained unhurt. Someone had spit on her shortly after we arrived but that was all.

Thursday night, however, the white members of N-VAC were talked into staying in the office—even Caroline, who was mad as hell at being segregated out of the riot. Then, driving into Watts, it began to look like nobody was going to make it; we encountered police barricades all around the "riot perimeter." We had to park the car and sneak in one or two at a time. We dropped off Woodrow, then Robert a block further down, then Danny Gray. The three of us who were left parked the car and, one after another, ran like hell across a street that formed the western perimeter. We kept running for a while and eventually found ourselves on a stretch of Avalon just south of Imperial—the area where rock throwing had started the night before. Police held the intersection where the Shell station was but were apparently not leaving their small, well-lit beachhead. Within a stone's throw of the police (literally) the crowd was able to break into stores, set fires and rip out pay phones—under the very eyes of the LAPD.

I stood outside timidly and watched for a police raid as my two friends joined the crowd in emptying a small grocery store. People were coming out with boxes and bags filled with canned goods. One man hung onto his hard liquor but set aside a case of Gallo sauterne to use as ammunition. Men were throwing bottles at street lights too to make the dark street darker. Until the lights were finally out, bottles kept crashing down on either side of the street, bringing startled and angry shouts. But there were no fights. Once, two kids started to square off but someone said, "Save it for whitey, brother," and they stopped.

Four or five hundred persons were roaming up and down that stretch of Avalon or were sitting on their apartment house steps. Women called to their kids to get inside. Teenagers were strolling around the block, shouting out to their friends, looking for news. There were cries—"Kill whitey," "Get whitey"—as well as a lot of talk: awed rumors of dead policemen, reports of other outbreaks on Central Avenue and on 103rd. People were proud as they began to realize the scope and force of what was happening. A woman said, "For the first time in my life, I'm proud to be black."

The looting itself was done with joy but it was no joke. Everybody wanted that food. I remember when

two men were carrying a carton of canned goods down
the street, people would come up to them: "Come on
brother, give me a can of something. Let me have those
peaches there. Just one can."

That evening one man looked at me and called out
angrily to the people around, "Is that a paddy?" (I'm
sort of in-between looking.) I shuddered and answered
quickly, "NO, brother!" He said, "Pardon me, brother,"
but I was sweating like a champ. I began to wonder if
this night's excursion might not be the worst mistake I
had ever made. What if someone didn't give me a
chance to say "NO, brother"? I walked over to find
Larry, who was a lot darker than me, and I never got
very far away from him for the rest of the evening.

The crowd swirled further south on Avalon to a
liquor store that was still open, its lights on. They called
for the clerk to come out: "Don't work for the white
man, baby. Join us." He didn't come out. Rocks went
through the glass front, then a broken-off stop sign,
finally a trash can. The clerk stayed inside while the
crowd begged him to come out. Then people pulled
back as someone shouted, "He's got a gun!" Finally the
clerk made it out the back door and everyone rushed in
through and over the broken glass. There was pan-
demonium inside the store but it was cleaned out in
minutes, first the money, then the hard liquor, then the
wine. Someone standing outside called out, "Goddamn
it, Louis, don't be choicy." My friends were very choicy.
They stayed in for several minutes and came out with
a hand-picked selection of Chivas Regal and other high-
ticket merchandise.

We were walking up Avalon again toward Imperial
when the police—30 or 40 of them—finally made a
flying raid down the street. The crowd disappeared immediately. I found it hard to run holding the four fifths
and a pint of Chivas Regal that I was supposed to
carry. I remember a series of back yards, holes in fences,
thorny bushes, as well as some fancy dodging to get
back across the perimeter. The pint had broken and I
could have gotten busted just for the way I smelled. It

was late. People were going home to party and to get ready for the next day.

On Friday we didn't have to travel. The rebellion spread to N-VAC's neighborhood on Central Avenue near 41st. Fires were burning all the way down Central. A clothing store on the corner three doors from us was broken into and persons of all ages were coming out of it loaded to the eyes with suits, shirts, hats and shoes. A few drove cars up and loaded them. There was the usual rush and flying glass but people were still choicy by and large. Many looked carefully for the right size, the right style.

Not long after the store had been completely emptied, four unmarked cars, filled with policemen, drove up. They stood with drawn guns around and inside the empty store. At one point, a boy of 14 or 15 came out of what looked like the store next to the looted one. He was unarmed and was carrying nothing. The police made a grab for him; he began running down the sidewalk where I was standing in front of the N-VAC office. The police fired several level shots down the sidewalk after him but fortunately missed him as well as those of us who were standing aghast on the sidewalk between him and the cops. The LAPD had always been free with their guns in the ghetto but this week they seemed to feel they had sanction to shoot people at will. Later I talked to a black cop who had previously been working in Hollywood and who had been a big booster of Chief Parker and his force. After three days' riot duty in Watts, my friend changed his mind. He told me about one man who was killed because he didn't raise his hands fast enough. And he told me that on one occasion he had been sitting in a temporary command post and heard two cops approaching who hadn't yet seen him sitting there. They were taking turns bragging about the niggers they had shot.

That evening we received word at the N-VAC office that a man was badly injured near 46th and Central and was getting no medical aid. Clay Carson, Robert

Hall and I took a first aid kit and began walking down
Central. We got past policemen by showing our N-VAC
cards and explaining what we were doing. When we
arrived at 46th the man was gone, so we started back
to the office. A policeman stopped us. We explained our
errand but he said he didn't give a shit what we were
doing; he waved his billy club and told us to turn back.
There was no point arguing. People were getting shot
for less. So we immediately turned around and began
walking away. The cop decided to get us anyway. He
clubbed Clay on the back of the neck and hit me on the
spine and on the back of my leg. I was knocked down
toward the sidewalk, which was covered with broken
glass, but managed to lurch forward and keep moving.

We finally got back to the N-VAC office and found
that a young friend, Danny Grant, had run into similar
trouble on Central. The cops had called him "nigger"
and "asshole" and had knocked him down and beat
him with their nightsticks. When we saw Danny, his
shirt was half-covered with blood and he was still bleeding from his forehead and mouth. We all stood around
in front of the office comparing notes and got hosed
down—accidentally, I guess—by firemen who were trying to put out a fire in the store on the corner.

That night I got to bed at about four in the morning.
It had been a hell of a day. I was exhausted but unable
to sleep. Instead I lay there, thinking about cops, and
let my mind go. Sometime close to dawn I caught myself in a little fantasy about how you would go about
killing every cop in Los Angeles. It was a lurid trip:
snipers, phony calls for help, howitzers and so on. I
caught myself, you understand. I'm nonviolent. I
wouldn't even step on a cop's toe. But here I was on a
mass murder trip. Then I thought about the previous
two years. Cops had dragged me around, called me all
sorts of nasty names, strangled me, kicked me in the
nuts, lied me into jail—and now today I'd gotten
clubbed and nearly shot. And I thought: yet and still,
I've had it easy. How do you feel when you've had it
worse? And what if you're not nonviolent—what if you

take violence for granted? What if you don't have that whole middle-class professional bag going for you? Then how do you feel about those uniformed thugs that occupy your community. Shit . . . most Americans can dig violence. In fact, they can even dig killing people they've never seen and don't know a damn thing about. They can say, "Oh boy, we wiped out 178 VC"—halfway around the world—and then those fools want to know why people are rioting in Watts.

I think it was Friday night that the Guard started to move in. I remember sitting in Celes King's bail bond office in the evening when they ran their Operation Clean Sweep down Central Avenue. There was a big loudspeaker telling everybody to get inside. Then there was a sort of parade that followed: some vehicles but mostly men marching with fixed bayonets. Someone was on the phone trying to keep track of the various N-VAC members. Celes and Robert Hall were in back having a little taste. The blinds were shut tight but several of us were curious and opened one slat a little to see what was happening. After a moment one soldier noticed the light and wheeled around, shouting and jabbing his bayonet toward the window. So we gave that up and I went back to join Robert and Celes.

Later, Woodrow called from Watts where there was still a lot of burning and looting going on. Parked cars had been overturned and set on fire. A good stretch of 103rd was going up in flames. Fastidious Woodrow had made his way through the broken glass into one drugstore but left emptyhanded when he found they were out of Viceroys.

The next afternoon we all got a better look when the National Guard made another sweep down Central. We kept inside the doorway of the N-VAC office—all except Danny Gray who walked out to hassle the Guard captain about something chickenshit the captain had called out to us. Danny kept his hands behind his head so that the Guard would have no excuse to shoot him and so that if they did, we would have a stronger case against them. Later, framed in the doorway, the troops marching down Central were like a newsreel of some army marching into a conquered city, with all its inhabitants off the street, peering out behind curtains and blinds. How weird. American GI's moving in . . . on us. We were Americans. Weren't we supposed to be out there in uniform, riding on tanks, taking snapshots, and passing out chewing gum and chocolate bars?

Sunday I left Central Avenue to represent N-VAC at a meeting that Governor Pat Brown had called with "Negro Leaders." N-VAC—a nonviolent group but still, in 1965, regarded as hotheaded militants—N-VAC hadn't been invited by the more respectable Negro Leaders who had arranged this meeting. But we decided to send somebody anyway.

The State Building was mostly empty. Out in front in the hot August sunlight were 30 or 40 suited and vested ministers, doctors, lawyers and political figures, who stood around chatting in quiet tones until the governor arrived. Then we were shown upstairs and through a series of rooms into a large elegant salon with a fireplace and soft carpeting. It was a hell of a room; everything in it murmured "dignity" and "responsibility." Governor Brown's in-person entrance and his attitude of casual good fellowship mellowed the atmosphere even more. We were a long way from Watts. And the governor, he treated us real good.

He spoke for a while. Let us know that he was on our side. But he also confided in us about some of his political problems—let us right into the picture. All about him and Mayor Yorty and Chief Parker and the Chandlers, who publish the *L.A. Times.* He seemed to be setting us up as "political realists" and almost everyone appeared willing to take on the role. Then, after a while, Brown explained that he hadn't come to make speeches and that he wanted to hear what we had to say.

The first speaker, Reverend Brookins, began with a

graceful encomium on Governor Brown as Friend of the
Negro. Then he briefly explained that "we" were asking for a blue-ribbon commission to investigate the situation. Brown in turn asked for suggestions for a chairman. A number of white men were named. One, I
remember, was Dean Acheson. Brown said that he himself had been thinking of Stanley (Mosk). John A.
McCone's name, incidentally, did not occur to anyone.

A little later Louis Lomax took the floor and talked
about the need for emergency food distribution, since
stores were either shut down or burnt out. Then a
series of reverends spoke about the need for Brown to
call upon all men of good will to work together to solve
this tragic problem that had beset us all. This Brown
was more than willing to do. Actually, he was being
put on as much as we were. The Negro Leaders arrayed
there were very reassuring, smiling urbanely, convey-
ing no sense of urgency, prescribing good will instead of
tea and toast, and a blue-ribbon commission instead of
fruit juices and lots of rest.

There was, however, one point when Brown showed
some uncertainty about the advice he was getting. He
asked, almost abruptly, if appointing a blue-ribbon commission would stop the rioting. There was an awkward
pause. I jumped up without being called on and
blurted out some of what I had seen and heard. I said
that if Brown really wanted to reach the rioters, he
would have to do it by some meaningful action—like
trying to put a leash on the LAPD. I suggested that
announcing a state attorney general's investigation of
LAPD practices in the past and during the riot might—
just might—have some meaning to the people who were
rioting.

Naturally, the governor didn't disagree. He just didn't
agree. He was amiable; in fact, he seemed to know
something about the cop problem in L.A.'s ghettos. But
he made no secret of his reluctance to antagonize the
vast Los Angeles electorate, so thoroughly brainwashed
by Yorty, Chief Parker and the Chandlers. It would
have taken courage for Brown to go after the police.

And that was clearly too much for "political realists" to ask.

The next day N-VAC started distributing food that we and CORE and other groups had collected all over the city. We turned the office into a small grocery store and gave away food all day to huge crowds of people who waited, sometimes for hours, in a line that often went halfway around the block.

The cops were busting people who had merchandise without a sales slip so we had to give out special slips with every bag of groceries. The police were getting really bad. One teenage girl working in the office borrowed my portable radio to listen to as she ran an errand down the street. She got stopped by a carload of shotgun-wielding cops who wanted to see the sales slip for the radio—which, incidentally, was weathered, cracked and had a broken antenna. They were taking her into custody for looting and she was in hysterics and unable to explain herself coherently when Danny Gray happened by. He recognized the girl and also my radio. So he ran back and got me and we went back to identify the radio. At that point they turned the girl loose and asked me where I got it. I said "At The Akron, six months ago." They demanded to see the sales slip. I agreed that it was certainly wise to carry sales slips for all of your possessions in case there might ever be a riot and you got stopped for looting but that, nonetheless, I didn't have one. Eventually, Danny and I managed to keep me from getting busted.

Back at the office the food was going out faster than it came in and there would be long waits and lengthening lines while people were out hustling donations. Some of it came from individuals; some of it came from supermarkets, bakeries and dairies which had developed a sudden interest in creating good will in the black ghetto.

Even after the local markets were open again, we managed to keep the food thing going for a few days. It was great—a kind of organized, legal looting. White housewives, bread companies and markets got rid of some surplus, and raggedy Central Avenue had a temporary windfall. Even when stores began to open, the lines didn't diminish—although the supply did. For mothers on welfare, for men out of work, it was still worth it to stand in the August heat for two hours on the chance of getting a free carton of milk or a loaf of bread.

Downtown, the governor's blue-ribbon commission was forming to investigate why black people would want to riot in Los Angeles.

THE DECLINE AND FALL OF EGOMEGALO

Ages ago on the tiny Mediterranean island of Egomegalo lived a people that took themselves and their
astronomy so seriously that they went to war with the
planets.

The people of Egomegalo believed, as did all of
Europe at that time, that Earth was the center of the
universe and that all the heavenly bodies revolved
dutifully around it. However, their astronomers couldn't
help but observe several troublesome objects in the sky,
which perversely refused to revolve around the earth.
These objects, which we call planets, took strange zig-
zag paths that could be fitted into an earth-centered
cosmology only by the most intricate and complex the-
ories.

The bleak and rocky hills of Egomegalo, however,
bred people of a more aggressive than theoretical nature. These islanders were more inclined to attack a
problem directly than theorize about it. They were, to
cut it short, fighters not thinkers. So they fashioned
bows so huge that it took four men to shoot each one;
they made the largest bows the world has ever seen.
And every night their best archers gathered in a square
at the center of the island's only town, aimed their
monster bows at whichever of the unruly planets were
visible, and shot scores of arrows into the night sky.
And shortly after each of these assaults, a rain of
arrows would descend on the island, sometimes on
fishermen's huts near the water, sometimes on the low
hills where sheep grazed and sometimes on the little
town itself.

The people of Egomegalo realized at once that the planets were retaliating, so the archers doubled their attack. More bows were built. More archers were enlisted and trained. Attacks were launched from every area of the island. But the brutal planets only fought back all the harder and with a more inhuman savagery. More than once an archer was struck down by the celestial counterattack before he had finished dispatching his own quota of arrows. The islanders realized that their first suspicions about the planets had been only too well founded. Such artisans as the island had were assigned to an emergency program of weapons development—and before long, a battery of enormous catapults had been devised, each catapult capable of hurling a huge boulder deep into the heavens. But the planets responded almost immediately with a sudden and vicious bombardment which killed several of the island people as well as a number of sheep, crushed one whole house and made the very ground shake.

Nowadays—when we know so much—it's hard to believe a people can have behaved so stupidly. Couldn't they see what was happening? They weren't primitive cave-dwellers after all. They had a well-developed technology and political system. They had arts. They were clearly civilized. In fact, in more than a few ways, they were like us.

The morning after the first boulder bombardment, two fishermen, who had lost their own boat, walked all the way into town and insisted to everyone who would hear them that the islanders were obviously not winning and would do better to scale down their assaults in the hope that the planets might do likewise. The fishermen were burned as traitors; everyone knew perfectly well that, without these assaults, which kept the planets weak, the island would have been totally devastated already.

In time the people of Egomegalo developed ways to hurl, first axe blades, then spiked iron balls, and finally boiling pitch into the sky—all at enormous velocity. It was felt that the planets were surely close to surrender.

But at the same time, the planets' treacherous and inhuman counterattacks were killing, wounding and scorching islanders by the score. Whatever race of evil creatures lived on the planets, they clearly had no regard for lives, neither their enemies' nor their own.

During this period one frightened islander, not too brave but clever for all that, managed to complete on his own a rough version of what our more enlightened century calls the "Copernican Theory." He argued to his fellow islanders that they were not the center of the universe after all and that the planets followed their own independent paths around the sun and were God's handiwork every bit as much as Earth. He pointed out that the planets, though undeniably cruel and barbaric in battle, might nonetheless be fighting out of fear. He argued that, if the islanders were to catapult up a peace offering—say a roasted ox or even a few bags of barley meal—the planets might then prove more friendly.

The brave people of Egomegalo, who were in no mood to listen to seditious nonsense, naturally burned this unfortunate theorist. One of their martial poets declaimed at the burning:

> Better to drink the nightly rain of boiling
>   pitch
> Than sip a sour peace in the suburbs of
>   Creation.

And the islanders went down, every last one of them, battling the insurgent planets.

HANCOCK PARK IN LATE DECEMBER

A shallow rivulet runs alongside your path from the parking lot on Curson to the County Art Museum. Between the path and the little stream a young woman in tight yellow bermuda shorts is stretched out on a blanket with her boyfriend. She's leaning on the boyfriend's stomach. She has blonde dutchgirl hair.

They sit up and kiss each other as I walk toward them on the path. Now she seems to be sucking his tongue. What I'd like to do is stand around and watch them for an hour or so; sooner or later, though, they'd notice me and they wouldn't take it well. So I walk on by. When I glance back, they've stopped kissing; he's squeezing a big handful of her ass.

About 25 yards down, there's a sturdy wooden bridge that sits heavily on the shallow trickle. Leaning on the bridge railing I can see the two tongue-suckers taking bottles of what looks like Nesbitt's Orange out of a plaid hamper. They've got some sandwiches too. The streamlet meanders from me to them through a slight valley in a mini-meadow adjacent to 6th Street and the Park La Brea Towers, halfway between Ohrbach's and May Co. The guy is wearing a white shirt, black sweater, brushed blue denims and blue sneakers. They look like a TV commercial now that they've stopped playing grabass and started consuming.

My path leaves the stream and takes me up a flight of stairs to the museum patio. Slouched down on a stone bench in front of the Ahmanson Gallery is a stoned couple; it looks like they may never move again. And you know, it's certainly possible that they've been doing a number or two but it's by no means necessary. A museum is its own special kind of trip. Never mind whether art is dead or not: everything inside a museum and everything around it too, trees, birds, people and all—they're all under a different, and a kinder, set of rules.

The gallery isn't open yet so I tour the trees in the patio. A small wind strikes up and I'm bombed by leaves: mustard-yellow leaves with saffron veins and speckles. It's a good tour. You dig the leaves and then you stand under that twisted triumphal arch they erected for the sculpture show and you look up the skirt of the fortyish lady sitting across from you. She has on a nicely plumped out black poor-boy top, red and green wooden beads, and shades. The view stops just short of where her stockings end but it's easy to picture the crumpled white flesh beyond and other good things. She's a groovy-looking lady. She would appreciate my digging her thighs.

The museum still isn't open so I walk out in front on Wilshire where the Peace and Freedom Party registrar is hustling voters with small success. And I call her a commie rat just to break the monotony for her. It does. But I'm still a little guilty for horsing around at art museums while peace and freedom are doing such rotten business on Wilshire Boulevard, not to mention everywhere else in the world.

From Wilshire you get a good view of the museum buildings rising out of a shallow lake of shit-brown water. This used to put me off, but not today. Because I had this dream last night. I dreamed I was alone in a chapel somewhere late at night. I felt, even though I'm a heathen, this enormous urge to kneel. Like if I kneeled, it seemed things would be just very very good. So I kneeled for a while and then went through a gate and up around the altar where there was a statue of the Madonna. She stood in some water which lay in a pool around her feet and then dropped into another pool, like one of those tacky continuous waterfall things you can get for $14.95.

Well folks I shit in that pool, or else I just wiped my ass and dropped the toilet paper in that pool. In any case it was something that would seem nasty by contemporary community standards. But not to me. I have to stress that. In my dream it seemed perfectly legitimate to me and I still felt very worshipful.

Then, however, a man came in—a sort of English actor. He had heard of me and was eager to meet me. All well and good. But then he didn't know about that shit up by the altar. And I got him out of the chapel trying to figure out how I could get back in there to clean things up. When I woke up, though, I thought: the hell with the Englishman. It was all right what I had done in the dream.

And so, for that matter, is the murky brown lake around the art museum all right. Why not? Crazy Jane says it in one of Yeats' poems: "Love has pitched his mansion in the place of excrement." If Love can pitch a mansion there, the museum trustees can goddamn well do it too.

The gallery has finally opened. And up on the third floor, Ruscha's Spam painting is already getting a lot of attention. The upper 2/5 of this painting is a field of dark blue with SPAM in huge yellow letters. The lower part is white canvas with scattered thin black streaks and a neatly rendered Spam can rocketing down across the canvas, leaving a flaring yellow exhaust behind it. The words "ACTUAL SIZE" are scrawled in the yellow flare. The painting is titled "Actual Size."

"Audrey, come here! How neat!"

Two little girls, delighted, are making a giggling unruly tour through the pop art section. It's their art. Some of the older people, however, take each canvas as a personal insult. Or they have learned to ask dreary bummer questions like "What is he trying to say?" and "Is it art?" All in all, the pop art room is a good place to rest. There's a couch in the middle; you can lean back and listen.

"Spam . . . I don't get much out of that somehow."

"Christ, I think I'll draw something and put it in here."

"Now THAT'S first-rate design."

"Spam! Haw!"

"It looks like a third grader did it."

"There's always some guys that take a can of Spam . . ."

Here come the Girl Scouts. They're walking through the museum in a column of two's. The scoutmother or whatever she is shrieks: "Girls, I want to see two lines. I do NOT want to see three." They come to a halt in front of Ruscha's painting. The scoutmother reads and explains:

" 'Actual Size'—See, that's an actual size can of Spam."

Finally I get up and leave pop art—walking past Renoir's plump bronze wife and over to the Monet "Water Lilies." It's a new canvas again; it is every time I come to it. Floating in murky brown water with a bile-green tinge are filmy luminous lily pads. They're pale blue green with here and there a little violet. Near the center of the painting are two bright creamy flowers flaring out of the flat watery plane. The lower flower has lots of yellow inside like melted butter, and the upper one has managed not just yellow but some crimson too, which edges its petals and tinges its center. Maybe everything in the world is a series of variations on that dream I had.

Monet, by the way, was in his 70's when he painted those water lilies. You won't believe this but he did it in a hobbies class at Art Linkletter's Sierra Dawn Retirement Homes.

Down three floors and a couple thousand years is my very favorite goddess: bright-eyed Athene, invincible warrior and lover of peace. Her statue is Actual Size at the very least—massive of thigh, moderate of bosom, with pretty, long toes and no arms at all. Elsewhere in the antiquities room I find a little boy, a little girl and their parents looking up at a towering Hermes with arms intact but with his marble wee-wee broken off.

Nearby in a colony of glass cases are Greek urns. They're lovely but they seem to have stopped giving interviews. And there, on one of them, is Hermes again, chasing a nymph, his wee-wee back on the job.

They've left a curtain open in the room, revealing a floor-to-ceiling window that looks out across the water to Wilshire. It's late afternoon already. The winter sun slants across all that brown water which comes right up to lap against the window. Sunlight glances off the rippling surface and makes a waterfall of trembling light across the ceiling of the antiquities room and down the wall on the other side. Beyond the water, the Peace and Freedom registrar is still there. People walk by her. The light is so strange and gray that it looks like a faded newsreel or even like something much older that I'm perhaps dreaming about. It's as though the antiquities room is now, and all that post-Christmas strolling and shopping is in the dead gray past. Inside, the little stream of shaking light overhead leads me across the room to the opposite wall where it tumbles on a thousand-year-old Japanese painting. It's Buddha, six-armed and seated in lotus position on top of a horse. Several men around the horse carry what looks like fruit in bowls. Buddha's hands hold scales, a skein of rope or cord, a bell. Two hands are in front of his chest, palms pressed together.

To walk out of the museum is an instant high. Everything is shapes and colors; the air is colder and fresher. The sky sits heavy on the tops of buildings; it hangs from the branches of trees; it fits, in snug inset fragments, among the leaves and twigs. Out by Wilshire the Peace and Freedom lady is still trying. Near her I lean on the rim of a massive circular fountain and get lost looking at the jets and hearing the water fall. Maybe if I'm here long enough, they'll put a plaque on me—"Untitled, 1935."

Behind the museum, Hancock Park is a field of tilted planes. The air is cold now walking back beside the streamlet, and smells like wet grass. It must be getting on toward dinner time and Madeleine will be off

work soon. The light's growing fragile. I can remember
a long time ago playing football on a damp lawn and
getting itchy from the grass but not noticing it until
the light got too dark to play in. Then you realized that
you were tired, scraped and streaked with green, and
that they were probably looking for you for dinner; the
air had gotten cold and you could smell wet grass.

The Student As Nigger—"For students, as for black people, the hardest battle isn't with Mr. Charlie. It's what Mr. Charlie has done to your mind."

The Student and Society—"It's astonishing that most students continue to see schooling as a privilege rather than a transaction in which they happen to be getting a rotten deal."

A Young Person's Guide to the Grading System—"History is so engrossing. Literature is so beautiful. And school is likely to turn them dull or even ugly. Can you imagine what would happen if they graded you on sex? The race would die out."

The Four-Fold Path to Student Liberation—"To be real in school is to be revolutionary."

Doing Time In New County—"At night after lights out we'd talk...you learned a lot in those aimless conversations: basic stuff like how many lids in a ki and how to strip a car—and more advanced techniques, like how to use the Escobedo decision, how to screw up a Nalline test, where to stash...."

PUBLISHED BY
POCKET BOOKS
PRINTED IN U.S.A.